HUMAN SOURCES

Managing Confidential Informants

John Buckley PhD

HUMAN SOURCES
Managing Confidential Informants

Acknowledgements

We will begin at the end and acknowledge the assistance of my dear friend Jenny Urquhart who made sure all my Ts were crossed and Is were dotted. There is little point in trying to do anything in intelligence, without enlisting the help of an analyst to make sure it is done accurately!

Then there is everyone else who kept repeating how badly I was doing things, until I learned to do them better. It is their knowledge that I am sharing here. A big thanks to them.

And to the human sources I have been fortunate to work with. Thanks for the hard lessons. But, please tell me I wasn't a complete ass, all the time!

iv

Contents

Forward

A few weeks ago, during this crazy COVID-19 world we are currently living in John and I connected for a chat. I asked John, "So what have you been up to?" His reply was "I have been writing. Two books actually." Yep, that's John. While the rest of us are trying just to stay somewhat healthy and alive, he is writing and learning. Despite feeling somewhat lazy and unworthy after hearing that I still agreed to write this forward.

I have known John for a decade when we first met at an International Association of Chiefs of Police conference when I was staffing the International Association of Law Enforcement Intelligence Analysts (IALEIA) booth. During the last 10 years we have worked together, travelled together, and become colleagues. I am also one of the lucky ones who has the privilege of calling John a friend, and he continues to be my mentor, my motivator, my biggest cheerleader, and my sounding board.

In this book and others he has written, John has the ability to mesh together scientific scholarly research and methodologies with real life scenarios, and examples. By doing so, he highlights not only the why you should employ a certain technique, policy or procedure but how. His use of metaphors, anecdotes and analogies help make the important points stand out. He provides flow charts and templates that will be useful in the real world. That is something often missing from texts such as this. But to be honest, there is extraordinarily little material available to practitioners about human source recruitment, development, and management. This book is a must read for anyone who aspires to work with human sources, currently works with human sources or manages those who do. It forces you to ask some hard questions, but more importantly, gives you some possible answers. It takes those previously taboo topics and puts them front and center.

If I am being honest, as a retired RCMP criminal intelligence analyst I have experience working on cases or heard of cases that illustrate just about every mistake that this book points out. John stresses the need for policy and procedure. It's not always sexy, but it is mandatory if we want to keep people safe and have successful prosecutions with bad guys in jail. Isn't that the result we are all hoping for? My hat is off to you John for continuing to take time to download all that awesome information from your busy mind and put it onto paper for those behind you. Your legacy continues.

Cheers,

Jenny

Jenny Urquhart Msc. CICA
Past President IALEIA
Royal Canadian Mounted Police (RCMP Ret'd)

Author's Note

The book continues work begun in 2000, in a United Kingdom Home Office Research Project that looked at better ways to recruit and manage human sources (confidential informants) (Reid and Buckley 2005). It continued into a book The Human Source Management System (2006) which identified psychological techniques that could be adapted for use in the field of managing human sources.

While that work attempted to shed new light on what, for the most part, was a very old business, the dearth of material previously written on the subject, meant it was only a beginning Since then it has become increasingly apparent that there were at least two obvious gaps in the material. First, these publications assumed that law enforcement agencies would have in place adequate structures that would facilitate using sources safely and ethically. Unfortunately, this is not always the case. Second, little attention seems to be paid to improving methods to maximize the amount of information we get from sources.

In short, law enforcement agencies are often taking risks they don't need to take, to obtain a limited amount of information. And some people seem happy with this.

Fortunately, I have the privilege of working with officers from different agencies, who are striving to improve how their agency manages human sources.

I often get to see how one agency is doing something well in one element but struggling in another, while a similar agency has the reverse.

What I have tried to do here, is bring together in one place, good practice, that has been collected from many different agencies. Hopefully, it will help reduce the mistakes we continue to make and improve the amount of information we get to protect our communities.

Not everyone will agree with what is written here. I have provided contact details at the end of the book and always welcome critique. Or if you are struggling to get buy-in from your agency, drop me a note and we will see if I can help.

I am sorry space has prohibited including more information here. If you want more related material, I have included details of five other books that will help you on your way.

And one final thing: the term 'confidential informant' is misleading and is only on the cover to appeal to a USA centric audience. Best to forget it.

John
London,
June 2020

x

The reason you despise me is that I can shine the light on what you truly are.

1. Finding a Better Way

Here is Edward Bear coming downstairs, bump, bump, bump, on the back of his head behind Christopher Robin. It is, as far as he knows, the only way of coming downstairs, but sometimes he thinks that there really is another way, if only he could stop bumping, for a minute to think of it.

The Complete Tales of Winnie the Pooh
- A A Milne

Introduction

It is a strange way to start a book on what is undoubtedly a very adult subject with a quote from a children's book. However, the quote in many ways captures the essence of what this book seeks to achieve. The child, Christopher Robin, is making his way down a staircase dragging, the almost as large as himself, Edward Bear behind, with the head of the poor bear bumping off each and every stair. There is no malice on the part of Christopher Robin it is just the way he has learned to do things and it works. It gets the desired result – Christopher gets to the bottom without losing the (more or less) still intact Edward. But as he gets there, he wonders to himself if there is another way of getting down the stairs without the necessity for all the head bumping? But the bumping doesn't stop for long enough to let him think.

When it comes to managing informants, we can carry on doing what we are doing with the bump, bump, bump of cases hitting the dismissed tray or the bump, bump, bump, of dead informants hitting the ditch, or we can change. What if there was a better way of doing it?

Beating around the bush

At this stage, we could go into a long palaver about the history of informant management, its rights, and its wrongs, etc. Instead, we are going to make two statements. If you agree with them; read on. If you don't, there is not much point; you will only get annoyed. First, managing informants is an essential aspect of effective law enforcement. Second, managing informants is a high-risk business that should only be carried out by professionally trained officers, working within a highly regulated system.

The content of this book is based on these two premises. Everything in the book is supportive of them. If we get the second one right, the first will happen.

The horse and the cart.

A bit of a conundrum in discussing any topic is the selection of the language to use and the reasons why we are using such language. If we give the reasons first, we can't use the right language. If we put the language first, the reader does not understand why that language is important. How can we explain why the horse goes in front of the cart if we don't know what a horse is and what a cart is?

Whether experienced or coming to the subject for the first time, the terminology used in the informant arena can be confusing. The terminology has evolved with various agencies using different terms for the same concept. This often leads to many of the problems we will discuss later. Identifying the terminology that will be used throughout the book will provide clarity for the reader from the beginning and make it easier to read. The following terminology will be used throughout this book:

'Registered Human Source' - Defined as: 'a person who has been deliberately recruited and is managed to collect information to satisfy an intelligence requirement.' (Reid and Buckley, 2005:18) This includes all individuals whether reporting on crime, terrorism, or espionage. The term 'source' will be used as an abbreviation. When considering the meaning of this many readers will be familiar with terms such as 'informant' which is widely understood by laypeople, 'covert human intelligence source' (defined in law in the United Kingdom) and 'confidential informant' a term widely used in The United States of America (USA). When you read the words human source it may help to think of a person registered as a confidential informant and everything that may entail.

'Human Source Management' - Defined as: 'the operational and social psychological process of recruiting and managing a human source to satisfy an intelligence requirement.' This term covers a broad range of activities surrounding the identification, development, and management of a human source. Throughout the book, this will be referred to as 'source management'.

'Handler' - Defined as: 'the officer who has day-to-day responsibilities for interaction with and management of a source.' This will often be an officer at the detective level but who, if the source is to be controlled properly, has received comprehensive training in how to manage sources.

'Controller' - This is the supervisor of the relationship between Handlers and source, and the relationship between the agency and the source. This is a term and a concept adopted from law enforcement in the United Kingdom. This will normally be a first-line supervisor for the Handler. Think: 'police sergeant.'

'Authorizing Officer' - This is the officer within the agency, who has the authority to register a person as being a human source for that agency.

Throughout the book, the terms Handler, Controller, and Authorizing Officer will all be capitalized. This is to draw attention to the fact that theirs is a designated role. They are not just *any* officer that happens to be doing the job.

'Agency' - The term agency describes a law enforcement body. This would include police services, other law enforcement agencies (e.g. Immigration and Customs, National Crime Agency, Federal Bureau of Investigation FBI, etc.) and Intelligence Services (e.g. Security Service (MI5) in the United Kingdom, Central Intelligence Agency CIA in the United States)

'Organization' - The term organization will be used to describe any group of people (3 or more) working together for a criminal purpose. The term embraces terrorist organizations, organized crime (such as Hells Angels, Mafia, etc) or a group of criminals that have come together to commit a single criminal act or acts (e.g. five ex-prisoners get together to commit a series of bank robberies.)

'Targeting' - Defined as: 'the process of researching an organization and/or individual to recruit a human source to satisfy an identified intelligence requirement.' This includes the collection of information that will facilitate the identification of a person's motives and a suitable method to maximize the potential for the successful recruitment of that individual.

'Recruiting' - Defined as: 'the process of establishing contact or a series of contacts with a person, to recruit them as a human source.' This process involves the building of rapport, the addressing of the identified motives, and the overcoming of obstacles that preclude recruitment.

'Handling' - Defined as: 'the post recruitment process that develops the person from being newly recruited to becoming a disciplined source who responds to instructions and tasks, in support of an intelligence requirement.' This includes the day-to-day management of the source at tactical and strategic levels.

'Criminal' - The term criminal is used to refer to an individual who spends the vast majority of their life involved in one criminal act followed by another. These periods of criminality are often interspersed with time spent in prison, an event that the individual comes to regard as an occupational hazard.

'Terrorist' - The term terrorist is defined as: 'any person involved in the commission, instigation or preparation of any act of terror for a political, religious or ideological cause.' This terminology is intended to be broad in scope, both regarding the role of the person concerned and the nature of the activity. The nature of the terrorist activity will include all actions that are designed to instill 'terror' in others including the victim of the crime. Ideology will include causes such as animal rights, anti-capitalism, anarchy groups, etc. that espouse their cause using violence.

'Target' - The term target refers to the subject of an investigation by a law enforcement agency. The term target will include both an individual and/or an organization. It should not be confused with the process of targeting which is defined above.

'Source Management Team' - The source management team consists of those officers of varying ranks with direct responsibility for the management of the source on behalf of the agency.

'Information to be considered for intelligence purposes' - The term 'information to be considered for intelligence purposes' is used to describe any material, communicated in any medium, to the agency or obtained by that agency in any way and which that the agency deems should be regarded as being of potential use for intelligence purposes. (Buckley, 2015) We abbreviate this phrase to 'information'.

'Intelligence' - Intelligence is a product, derived from the movement of information through an agreed process, which is created to assist in the prevention or investigation of crime and/or for national security (Buckley, 2015). We collect information. We process that information and create intelligence. Sources give us information, not intelligence.

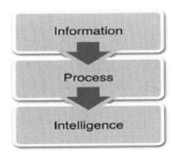

Figure 1.1 Information/Intelligence

'Intelligence requirement.' - An intelligence requirement is a request from a decision maker for intelligence relating to the subject specifically identified in the requirement. It is the responsibility of those receiving the request to collect and process information into intelligence, to satisfy that request. The identification of intelligence requirements and the collection and processing of the required information are integral steps of the intelligence cycle.

'Technique' - The term technique refers to 'a behavior or series of behaviors employed by a person to achieve the desired outcome'. Throughout the book, we will discuss techniques that can be used to manage a source. Essentially techniques are tools to do the job. We want officers to have as many options as possible at their disposal.

Knowledge management

Given the fact that we have already stated that this book will address what may be considered by many to be basic tactics involved in managing sources, it would be foolish not to address the subject of 'knowledge management'. Knowledge includes the understanding of a context and having insights into the relationships within that context. It also includes the ability to identify opportunities and problems within the context and provides the ability to predict the implications of future actions. It is about knowing stuff and knowing what to do with the stuff we know.

Knowledge management is about finding a way to store or maintain knowledge collectively within the corporate memory. It is about putting in place systems to make sure that knowledge that is often hard-won is both shared with other staff and not lost to future generations.

In the context of managing human sources, knowledge management is at best poor. The secretive nature of the work means that many of those engaged are reluctant to commit to paper methods they have developed, understandably not wishing the 'enemy' (criminals, terrorists, hostile nations) to become aware of what is being done. Unfortunately, this lack of knowledge management creates a set of circumstances where significant learning is lost, mistakes are repeated and those new to the business, spend years acquiring the knowledge that already existed. To compound, this problem is the reluctance of many to engage in any form of research to develop new or better methodologies. The loss of knowledge is exacerbated, in some jurisdictions, by a reluctance to devote enough resources to training, that is specifically tailored to meet the demands of the role. What this leads to is stagnation within law enforcement, who then fail to utilize the knowledge that had been gained by their now-retired colleagues. This book is about knowledge management. It is about capturing the things that officers have learned over many years and sharing it with others.

Book structure

The book is designed to be read from start to finish, as each chapter builds towards the next. The reader can then revise different aspects at their leisure. Unless you are gifted with an incredible memory and intellect, it is highly unlikely that you will be able to assimilate all the information in one reading, let alone apply it in an operational environment. It is acknowledged that readers will have different levels of experience and in some parts, it may appear to be stating the obvious. However, in research carried out for the book it became apparent that what may appear to be obvious to some, is far from obvious to others. Furthermore, some of the content may challenge long-held beliefs and if the reader disagrees with what is written then that is their prerogative.

Many of the issues raised are likely to apply to other intelligence-gathering processes such as the use of undercover officers, surveillance, and the interception of communications. Whilst all these activities are intrinsically linked or should be, to the activities of a source the specifics of such operations will not be addressed save for the use of sources in such operations.

Transnational understanding and confusion

One of the many problems in attempting to establish what is good practice when it comes to managing sources is the plethora of terminology used to describe sources, compounded by often ambiguous interpretations of what the law enforcement agency envisages a source to be. If we intend to maximize the benefits that law enforcement obtains from sources, then we must start by having clarity around their role. As the United States Senator S I Hayakawa said:

> *"If we allow certain keywords in our vocabulary to remain undefined, we tend to project an illusion of meaning that ultimately hinders and misdirects our thinking."*

Such differences in terminology occur not only between jurisdictions but often between agencies within those jurisdictions and within agencies themselves. Terminology differences between nations are understandable given both the nature of language and the different judicial systems. Differences within a nation or a specific agency are indicative of and driven by egocentric behavior, and a lack of willingness between agencies to give up their fiefdoms and find a compromise for a common good. Such behavior creates poor operational practices and is counterproductive when it comes to developing and sharing good practice.

The purpose of discussing such differences here is to illustrate that regardless of how much individuals and agencies develop good techniques to manage sources, ultimately much will be lost because those techniques are used in isolation and not shared or adapted within the wider law enforcement/intelligence community. Let us illustrate some of these differences:

United Kingdom: Legislation in the United Kingdom (UK) has provided all involved in managing sources with the term 'Covert Human Intelligence Source (CHIS)' and with it a standard, if tortuous, definition of the behavior that must occur for a person to become a CHIS. The mandated behavior relates to both the individual and the agency. Once a person is categorized as a CHIS they must be managed by the agency under the relevant legislation and follow nationally set standards. Defining a CHIS and providing a legislative basis for their use was primarily driven by the adoption of the European Convention on Human Rights (ECHR) and its adoption into UK legislation. The path to standardization within the UK has not been an easy one with many discussions around when an individual, falls into the CHIS category, and when they don't. From a practical perspective, it is inferred that when an agency undertakes to register a person as a CHIS, then the agency intends to engage with that person regularly, over an identified period and towards identified objectives.

Europe: Many European countries are adopting similar methods and terminology used by UK law enforcement. This has come about for several reasons including the significant amount for transnational investigation within Europe, the need for compliance with the European Convention on Human Rights and other doctrines established by the European Union, and perhaps in a more promising sense, the genuine desire of law enforcement to establish and share good practice throughout the region.

Canada: Within the Canadian criminal justice system two terms predominate that of 'source' and 'agent' with both being considered as a type of informant. The distinctions between source and agent are intended to be legally clear but often leads to a degree of confusion both practically and when it comes to the evidential process. Both sources and agents provide law enforcement with information about criminality. However, there are two main differences. First, it is argued that law enforcement cannot 'task' a source to obtain information. An agent can be tasked. This can lead to confusion around what constitutes tasking with the rules being bent to meet the agency's needs. Second, and most importantly, once someone becomes an agent, then they also become a compellable witness, and all records associated with the case are subject to the discovery/disclosure process in any subsequent prosecution. In effect, the agency knows from the start that the 'agent' will be giving evidence but also knows they will have to look after that individual for a considerable period after the prosecution. There are benefits to this way of working but the downside is the long-term (perhaps a lifetime) engagement with that agent post-trial.

United States: In the United States the most frequently used term is that of confidential informant with most agencies using this term, notable exceptions being the Central Intelligence Agency (CIA) which favors the term 'HUMINT' and the Federal Bureau of Investigation which has more recently adopted the term 'confidential human source'. While outwardly the widespread use of the term confidential informant may appear as having benefit, it is not until we start to look at the wide variance in definitions used throughout the US criminal justice system that we realize how disparate the meanings are. The term confidential informant frequently embraces many different circumstances in which people pass information to law enforcement including contexts as diverse as the school teacher passing on a piece of information on drug consumption in the environs of a school, a member of a drugs cartel giving details of drugs importations, a member of terrorist gang reporting on terrorism and a person giving evidence to receive a lighter sentence. This confusion of terminology and the associated roles of the individuals involved, has led to significant criticism of law enforcement (Natapoff, 2009) and arguably has contributed to the 'stop snitching' campaign that has become prevalent in many US cities. The widespread disparity in the definition within a jurisdiction means that many agencies are likely to be impacted when one agency makes errors. For example, the introduction of Rachael's Law came about following the tragic death of Rachel Hoffman in Tallahassee, Florida in 2009. (See: Florida Statute 914.28 Confidential informants.) More importantly, where there is widespread confusion about what constitutes an informant it becomes extremely difficult to identify the best way to manage the relevant individuals and mistakes become commonplace.

Australia and New Zealand: The term 'Human Source' is now the most common description used. Whilst definitions may vary from agency to agency, there is a shared understanding as to what constitutes

14

a human source. However, in many cases, people are still registered as human sources when in effect they have supplied information on a one-off basis.

Categories.

Within individual agencies, a plethora of terms is often used to try and cover the different circumstances in which a person provides information to law enforcement. Terms such as confidential informant, informer, informant, casual contact, confidential source, confidential contact, agent, CHIS, human source, and even witness, are often used interchangeably by members of the same agency. Not only does this lead to much confusion it means the limited resources of the agency are often wasted with needless bureaucracy. More seriously, it can often mean that people who put themselves at risk by providing information are not properly protected by the agency.

When it comes to passing information, law enforcement needs to identify and use specific named categories into which they can place the individual who is supplying information. When placed in the identified category the agency can then manage that individual according to an agreed and documented set of standards. Using identified categories and working to agreed standards ensures that the risks to the person and the agency are managed effectively. This will also ensure that there is legal compliance.

There are three categories that we can use as a starting place for someone who is giving information to an agency:

1. **Registered Human Source.** As defined above: '*A person who has been deliberately recruited and is managed to collect information to satisfy an intelligence requirement.*' This term refers to a person with whom an agency enters a relationship, to obtain information, over an identified period, and under a specified set of circumstances. This relationship is authorized by an Authorizing Officer, and all aspects of that relationship are documented. This person is managed only by trained and designated officers.

2. **Tasked Witness.** This term refers to a *person with whom the agency enters into a relationship with the intention that the person will give evidence in court against another person.* Such a person may or may not be serving a prison sentence at the time of passing the information. The person knows they will be testifying. The tasking aspect of this term refers to where a person is to be used clandestinely for a limited period to gather further evidence. Inevitably there will be a cross over with the activities of a registered human source, but the intention is always that they will testify before a court. However, in the early stages, their identity probably requires protection. In the USA this would include what is referred to as 'jailhouse informant.' Such an

individual is often tasked to elicit a confession from a cellmate in return for a lighter sentence.

3.   ***Member of the Public.*** This term refers to all other persons that do not fall within either Category 1 or 2 above and refers to *'any person passing information to the law enforcement agency in the expectation that their identity remains confidential',* This means that the intention of the agency and the desire of the individual, is that their identity will be protected except when there is a legal requirement to disclose it. For ease of use, we may refer to these people by the acronym 'MoP'. (Buckley 2009)

With both registered human sources and members of the public the premise should always be that their identity is protected in law under what is known in many jurisdictions as 'informant privilege'.

Inevitably, it is not always possible to divide people into such distinct categories. There are rules of thumb we can use to see where a member of the public (MoP) fits in when it comes to them passing information to law enforcement. First, does the person want their identity to be kept confidential? If the answer is 'yes' they will fall into the category of registered human source or a member of the public. Second, if the intention is that the person is entering into an extended relationship with the agency, they will be a registered human source. Third, if the person is giving information regularly, they will be a registered human source. A good guide is that if a person gives information three or more times in a year-long period, then an assessment should be carried out by a Controller to see if they should be registered as a human source. Fourth, if the person is being tasked to gather information, they will be a registered human source.

These rules apply whether the person giving the information is a saint or a sinner. Generally speaking, when it comes to deciding if a person is to be treated as a source or a MoP, the deciding factor is the number of contacts they have with police over a year. However, if a criminal is passing information on an ad hoc basis, there will be many additional risks and it is prudent of the agency to let trained officers speak with this person. Many officers are corrupted through such relationships because they do not have the training to see what is happening and the agency does not have structures in place to protect them. Where people are obligated under law to pass information to law enforcement, for example, banks or medical professionals, an identified system should be put in place to manage this process. In many jurisdictions taking such information outside of a stated process may break data protection laws. And on the topic of data protection legislation, we cannot phone our cousin in the travel agency to see where our target is flying to. This is likely to break the law. Hiding our actions by saying our cousin was a source offers no protection unless they are registered as such, and the activity authorized.

Law enforcement agencies need to make these distinctions to protect everyone involved, the judicial process, and the reputation of the agency. As we will see manging sources safely and productively takes a lot of time and resources. An agency simply does not have enough resources to manage everyone who gives them information, in the same way. We don't put the same resources into investigating a stolen bicycle as we do into investigating a murder. The concepts are similar. There will always be some crossover in how these people are managed and the records which are kept.

Before progressing any further, it is worth discussing if a person who has been managed as a source should at a later time be used as a witness. Generally speaking, the answer to this is a strong **NO**. Everything we have done before with the source is likely to come under scrutiny and any convicted person that has ever been in contact with the source before that date, that is now in prison is likely to call foul and allege they were set up by the source. Furthermore, it may expose covert methodology that should not be exposed. If we want to use a person clandestinely to gather evidence, then two things should be done. First, the person should be managed by a trained Handler and an Investigator. The Handler protects the source and supervises all covert activities and the Investigator ensures that all activities comply with evidential standards. They also identify where there may be problems with disclosure during the court process. Second, all records are kept to evidential standards, and officers and the source make written statements as the investigation progresses. These are not left to the last minute. Table 1.1 provides a general view of the differences between sources, tasked witnesses, and MoPs.

	Common Description	Informant privilege	Obligation to Protect Their Life	Managed by
Registered Human Source	Confidential Informant (USA) Covert Human Intelligence Source (UK) Source (Canada)	Yes	Yes	Trained Officer
Tasked Witness	Jailhouse Informant (USA) Cooperating Witness (UK) Agent (Canada)	No	Yes	Trained Officer
Member of the Public	Confidential Contact Casual Source	Yes	Yes	Any Officer

Table 1.1 Differences in Role

Names matter

Words are important. Throughout this book, we use the term 'registered human source' to describe the person who is giving us information (abbreviated for convenience to human source or source). Acknowledging that the term confidential informant is widely used, there are reasons why we have elected to use the term registered human source and they are worth discussing. Those wishing to make changes within their agency can then speak from a position of knowledge. First, the term confidential informant has different meanings to different people. This creates confusion for everyone and ambiguity regarding how the person is managed. For example, one agency may regard a nosey neighbor who phones the police naming youths for disturbing the peace as a confidential informant, while in the same agency a detective is collecting information from a person deep within an organized crime gang. The agency also regards this person as a confidential informant. Most officers will be able to deal satisfactorily with the first situation; very few with the second situation.

Second, the word informant has many negative connotations. Often, the people passing the information don't want to be viewed as an 'informant'. In addition, many officers receiving the information have negative views of an informant, and the general public, as a rule, despise informants. The word source is a more neutral and more professional choice.

Third, by using the term human source the inclusion of the word human emphasizes that the person is fundamentally no different from any other person. Their wants, needs, and desires are going to be the same as ours, and how they behave in a given set of circumstances is going to be similar to how we would behave in those circumstances. Human beings are the same the world over. Referring to these individuals as human sources, enables us to have a better understanding of their behavior. This makes the presumption that we have been trained in understanding human behavior.

Fourth, the word 'registered' is included to indicate to all involved the status of this person within the agency, and to emphasize that that person falls under the agency's regime for the management of sources.

Fifth, many of the terms used to describe people who give information are deliberately offensive and designed to deter people from giving information. Included are terms such as Snitch, Rat, Narc, Gig, Grass, Tout, and a plethora of others. It is bad that the general public uses them but unprofessional if officers do. Slang terms or derogatory language should never be used to describe a source. The use of such language conveys the mindset and values of the officer using them. If an officer thinks in these terms, they will behave accordingly.

Competing needs

Now that we have identified our terminology, we can start to look at what we have to do to manage a source. We will begin by looking at the issue from the perspective of the source. Figure 1.2 illustrates how the source will be pulled in different directions because of their role.

Figure 1.2 Competing Needs

The first aspect that we will look at is the needs of the agency. When we talk about agency needs what we are referring to is what the agency wants from the source (information) and the legislation, policy, and procedures, and resources that limit their actions. The second aspect is the safety needs. There are physical risks in managing sources, to the officers involved, to the source, and the public. Managing sources endangers people's lives. Every meeting with a source creates a risk to their safety. They may be reluctant to risk it often. The third aspect is the needs of the source. These will revolve around psychological needs including how they feel about what they are doing, their relationship with the Handlers, and their motives for providing information. Understanding the social psychology involved here is critical for the Handler.

Now let us look at a few examples of how conflicts will arise. An agency may want the source to produce many arrests and seizures but does not have the financial resources to reward the source. An officer may want to search a source to see if the source is armed; the source may say no. The Handler may offend the source, thereby damaging the relationship and demotivating the source.

Understanding the source's psychological needs is critical to the effective management of the source. Good Handlers put a lot of effort into addressing these needs. Others rely on coercion. This book is dedicated almost exclusively to ensuring that the structures are in place to address the agency's needs. Only if, and when, these are in place, is it safe to even consider manging a source.

Common problems

Many law enforcement officers continue to hold the misguided opinion that sources belong to them and not to the agency. These mistaken beliefs occur for several reasons, many of them are human failings. First, officers are often judged on how productive they are and if the officer has access to a good source, then they are far more likely to get results and the related praise from management. Second, and not unrelated to the first, is that if an officer is managing a good source and getting results, then they are likely to be held in greater esteem by colleagues, providing them with kudos and satisfying the needs of their ego. Third, not every officer can recruit and manage sources, and many are unwilling to make the effort to do so. The potential exists for an officer to see others, who are lazier or less capable, reap the benefits of their efforts if they share the information 'their source' has provided. Fourth, and from a much more worrisome perspective, some officers use the lack of control over source relationships within an agency, to mask inappropriate behavior. This behavior can be as innocuous as dodging out of the office for an hour 'to meet a source', to the more sinister behavior, of covering a wholly corrupt relationship be it sexual, or criminal.

From an agency perspective, this mindset should be eliminated. A failure of the agency to put in place adequate systems is likely to create problems including, an increased likelihood of officers becoming involved in an inappropriate or corrupt relationship. There will be a failure to afford adequate protection to the source resulting in harm to the individual and allegations of negligence, or a lawsuit. There will be a waste of agency resources with officers spending significant amounts of time meeting sources who are not making any significant contribution to the strategic or tactical demands the agency has set. There will be good prosecution cases lost, because of the exclusion of evidence when doubts are raised by defense counsel about the involvement of a source. The full benefits of the source will not be realized. Sources will not produce the quantity and quality of information that they have the potential to access because the Handler will only ask about the topics that the Handler is interested in. The agency should have the benefit of being able to deploy the source to help in other investigations. These are the overarching problems but if we drill down into the weeds, we will encounter many more problems that occur in source relationships. Here are some of the common ones:

- Creating false information to justify action against another party. For example, making up information to justify search warrants.
- Submitting only part of the information provided by the source. This may be done as a deliberate act or through laziness.
- Managing sources 'off the books.' The officer knows the person is a source, and the source believes they are a source, but the officer does not inform the agency of the existence of the relationship.
- Putting undue pressure on someone with mental health problems or other similar vulnerability, to become a source.
- Theft of money intended for the source or to be used in the management of a source.
- Both consensual and non-consensual sexual relationships with a source.
- Maintaining a relationship where there is a personal gain for Handler, such as free tickets for football games, free drinks at a bar, etc.
- Unauthorized meetings by the Handler with the source and/or a failure to report telephone contacts.
- Failure by management to provide equipment or training intended to protect the source relationship.
- Failure by those involved to notify senior management of the risks to the safety of the

source. This often occurs because source safety is competing with another agenda which the officer deems more important such as 'making the case.'

- Failure by senior management to acknowledge or address risks raised to them.
- Reckless disregard for fieldcraft by those handling the source. This will include such things as not using defensive surveillance or meeting a source in a location that is dangerous for the source because it is more convenient for the officer.
- The reckless disclosure of a source's true identity by Investigators or prosecutors.
- Managers, turning a blind eye to wrongdoing either consciously or because 'It's just too difficult to deal with.'
- Officer's claiming to have sources that don't exist, to boost a promotion application.
- Management using the number of sources as some sort of performance criteria.

All these issues stem from one fundamental problem – a lack of understanding about how to manage human sources safely and effectively.

The law

As this book is intended to be used by officers managing human sources in many countries it will not address most of the complex issues regarding legislation and sources. However, two legal issues are relevant in every country. First, that of protecting the life of the source and second, when there is a connection between information that a source has provided and subsequent legal proceedings.

When it comes to protecting the life of a human source many different pieces of legislation will come into play including human rights legislation and workplace safety legislation. It can take a significant amount of legal understanding and the study of relevant case law, to interpret the legislative nuances that apply when it comes to managing sources. Most officers do not understand them. However, we can simplify it as follows: The agency should not do anything or omit to do anything, that leads to the death of, or injury to, a source as a result of their role as a source. This includes taking all *reasonable* measures to protect the source's life. Poor structures, poor training, poor fieldcraft are the types of *negligent* behavior that lead to sources being killed. Revealing the identity of a source to too many other law enforcement officials, including prosecuting staff, is another big factor.

The second issue relates to why we often use sources. We want to bring the guilty to justice. We want to arrest perpetrators and bring them before the courts. What we are trying to do is turn information, into intelligence, into evidence. How we go about this can lead to compromising the source and/or the prosecution. There are two main interrelated issues when it comes to using information from a source in a court case. First, we are obligated under the law and ethically to protect the identity of the source from being exposed as a result of the prosecution. Second, the way that the source's information has been used in the investigation may mean it has to be disclosed to the court, and ultimately to the defense lawyers.

With the first of these, internationally, courts agree about the necessity to protect the identity of sources. There is case law in many jurisdictions, dating back for over a hundred years, that recognizes that law enforcement needs to use sources and that the identity of the source should be protected. This concept is commonly referred to as 'informant privilege'. As a baseline, informant privilege says we don't have to say who a source is, and we have the court's backing on this. Except...

The second of the issues connected with protecting a source's identity is the exception to the informant privilege rule. It is commonly referred to as the 'innocence at stake' rule. In short, if a person is unable to prove their innocence without knowing the identity of the source, then the identity of the source must be revealed. Where an accused person establishes that information exists that could raise a reasonable doubt as to their guilt, and that information is not available in any other way than through identifying the source, the source's identity must be revealed. Some courts take a very liberal interpretation of this principle, leaning heavily towards the accused, despite the obvious jeopardy to the life of the source should their identity be revealed. Some defense lawyers exploit this rule knowing that law enforcement will be reluctant to jeopardize a person's life. The argument then becomes, give up your source or give up your case. As a tactic, this works but it does not serve justice.

Where the innocence at stake rule can often be exploited comes from how the source's information has been used in building the case. The most common instance is when information has been used to obtain a search warrant. Where evidence has been gained from a search that is prejudicial to a defendant, a lawyer will often try to establish that the warrant was unlawfully obtained, and by default, all evidence stemming from the search must be excluded. 'My client had drugs in the house, but the police should not have found them. They should not have been there because their warrant was unlawful.' This technique to exclude evidence is often referred to as 'the fruit of the poisoned tree.' The poisoned tree being the warrant and the fruit is the evidence that was subsequently found, when the warrant was executed.

A further benefit for the defense is that the more the 'reliability' of the source is questioned the greater chance their identity will be revealed, thus creating a predicament for the prosecution: defend the warrant by disclosing the source's identity or lose the evidence. This type of situation should be predicted before the case ever goes to court and decisions made at the highest level within the agency in consultation with the prosecutor. The question being decided is: Will the life of the source be placed in jeopardy? And, if their life is placed in jeopardy, what obligations have we then to protect that life, and how can we do it? Giving the source a one-way bus ticket is not the answer. We will return to the subject of source 'reliability' in a later chapter.

The duty to provide any evidence which might undermine the prosecution case or aid the defense case is commonly known as *disclosure*. The prosecution must disclose to the defense any material that fulfills these criteria. Unfortunately, officers often don't know or don't understand the law about what can be discovered and what must be disclosed. They are also unsure under what circumstances concepts such as 'public interest immunity' can be invoked to protect 'sources and methods.' Also, some officers are lazy, all they want is a quick result, and the actions they take make it easy for the person charged to identify the source. Professional Handlers know their legislation and the case law relevant to source management and use this knowledge to protect the source's identity. Protecting methods is also important. Similar methods are used to manage sources across the world. Some of the techniques used to protect the source are extremely sensitive. If these are exposed in one courtroom, it does not take long for that knowledge to spread through the criminal fraternity, making it harder for everyone involved in law enforcement. If we mess up and disclose sensitive methods, we mess it up for the whole law enforcement community. If we mess up and disclose a source's identity, we may be responsible for their death. Pulling a case versus protecting the source's identity, is a common ethical dilemma. While ethics training will help in addressing this dilemma, good handling of the source and proper investigation strategies will reduce the chances of the dilemma arising in the first place.

The need for legislation

It is beneficial for law enforcement if the jurisdiction in which they are operating has introduced good legislation regarding the management of human sources. Such legislation provides clarity that protects civil liberties and provides clarity around what can and cannot be done. It should also make clear what the obligations are on law enforcement regarding protecting the source's life. The difficulty is getting the legislatures to write legislation that is both effective and practical. Including laws that make it all but impossible to carry out the work, just means that either a legitimate law enforcement technique is removed from their arsenal, or officers find a way to bend or work around the law. Consultation between law enforcement source management experts and legislatures is essential in drafting any law. If it is left to lawyers, bad law will result.

Fieldcraft

Fieldcraft refers to the techniques deployed by the source management team to ensure the safety of all parties when they are meeting with a source. It addresses the safety needs component of Figure 1.2 above. It is sometimes referred to as tradecraft though that term has several meanings. It includes techniques taught to a source so that they may protect their safety at all times. Many of these techniques are sensitive and their compromise would endanger the lives of the source, their family, and the officers involved in managing them. As such these techniques have to remain protected from public discussion. Notwithstanding this, several points can be made.

Fieldcraft training (discussed in Chapter 2) should be mandatory for all officers involved in managing a source. The importance of this type of training cannot be emphasized enough. Unfortunately, many officers are over-confident in their ability to keep themselves safe during a meeting. In addition, agencies do not provide sufficient training in these matters because the risk to the source is not properly identified or because the agency is complacent about the safety of the source. A failure to provide this type of training to officers is *negligence*.[1] A failure to utilize the training recklessly endangers both the life of the source and the officers involved, and potentially other citizens.

---

[1] When discussed throughout the book negligence is to be considered within in its legal meaning. Negligence occurs when someone injures or causes a loss to another because of their careless or reckless behavior. Negligence can include a lack of care for the consequences of one's actions or using less care than that of a reasonable person.

2. A Systematic Approach

It is impossible for a man to learn what he thinks he already knows.

Epictetus (50-135 AD)

Introduction

In this chapter, we will look at the structures that are necessary to manage human sources safely and effectively. This will include everything that is needed in terms of policies, roles, and training. It will also discuss where the management of sources interconnects with the wider aspects of intelligence management. While we intend to show best practices, it is recognized that for some agencies there will be difficulty in implementing some of what is suggested here. This is not because what is suggested is undoable, it is because there needs to be a will at a senior management level to implement change. As a word of encouragement, if we can get one leader to make the changes, the benefits of change become readily apparent to others. Everything that is suggested here is intended to increase the amount of information we obtain from human sources. Despite what we often hear from naysayers, managing sources with significantly less risk does not decrease productivity, it does the opposite. It is just that in the process of change some egos take a bit of a bashing and some people who portrayed themselves as being the 'best' are left looking like the emperor with no clothes.

34

There are likely to be five categories of people with regard to any innovation (Rogers 2003). First are the visionaries. These are the people with vision. They have a high tolerance for risk and regularly interact with other professionals to seek new knowledge about their business area. They will identify that change is needed and suggest solutions. They are likely to be creative but need a steadying hand. They make up about 2-3% of the workforce. Holden Ford, in the Netflix series Mindhunter, is a good example. Staying with this series we can see the steadying and more political influence is provided by his colleague Agent Bill Tench. He is a good example of the next category 'early adopters'. Early adopters see the need for change and take a judicious approach to adopt it. They make up about 10%. These are the people that need to be on board in the agency, if a change is to occur. Particularly what is needed is someone in senior management who can lead it and navigate the politics. These are the people that will make the change happen. The third category of people making up about 35%, is the early majority. These people will buy into the change at various times in the process. Once convinced of the benefits these people are happy to engage it. After this comes the late majority, making up another 35%. These individuals are generally skeptical of anything new, and any change does not sit well with them. However, after a bit of huffing and puffing, they can be convinced and will comply. The final category making up about about 15%, are people referred to as laggards. These are the ones that will actively fight any change. They are likely to have invested heavily in the old way of doing things and have a lot to lose with any change, not least their position or status. They fear what change will cost them personally and will use every tactic at their disposal to undermine the changes. They are potentially destructive in any agency. Which one are you when it comes to managing human sources?

The foundation

Three pivotal elements are needed if human sources are going to be managed effectively. Without them, everything else is for naught.

Figure 2.1 Human Source Management Platform

The first element is made of ***policy and procedures***. Policy and procedures set out how the agency is going to carry out its business. The second element are ***records***; the records the agency keeps of what has happened. The third element is ***training***; the training the agency provides to those officers involved in the role. We will explore what is needed in policy and procedures, and what are the training requirements here, and explore what records are needed in Chapter Three.

Policy and procedures

No human source management system can function properly without good policies and comprehensive procedures. The terms 'policy' and 'procedure' are often used interchangeably again creating confusion among users. Throw in the term *'guidance'* (discussed later) and it makes for a broken system. Understanding the difference in each is important if the agency is to avoid being left vulnerable to corruption, poor performance, and public criticism. To begin, it is important to note that the law, be it federal, state, or local statute and any attendant documents cannot be surpassed by policy or procedures. While this may seem obvious it is surprising how many law enforcement policies conflict with legislation, normally because the policy has been written by someone who has not been trained in writing policies and procedures. Let us begin by clarifying what we mean by the terms policy and procedures.

A policy is a statement of an agency's intentions to discharge their obligations to the public, concerning a particular business area. It states an intention to carry out certain functions and provides parameters about those functions. A policy establishes limits to action. They will of necessity be public documents and signed off by the Chief of the agency. A policy is normally brief. It does not require detail.

Procedures outline a method of performing an act or a manner of proceeding on a course of action. They differ from a policy in that they direct a member of the agency how to act in a particular situation, and how a specific task should be performed. Procedures must be comprehensive and explain to the reader what they should do in the vast majority of circumstances they are likely to meet. Procedures are constructed from the knowledge of individuals operating in the business area. Formalizing this knowledge means that good practice is identified and perpetuated long after such individuals have left the agency. With procedures, this knowledge is set out in a structured format agreed by senior management and goes a long way to eliminating mistakes that have been made in the past. One of the unfortunate aspects that occur with procedures is that the reason why a particular procedure was put in place is often forgotten with time. Those currently involved then mistakenly believe that it is alright to deviate from or change, that procedure. They fail to realize that they are removing a measure that was put in place to achieve a certain goal or objective, or to prevent a risk that would potentially materialize. Procedures should be linked to an agency's discipline regulations so that members who deviate from them without cause, can be held fully accountable and face the consequences for their actions. Procedures can be deviated from, but any member doing so must be held fully accountable for their actions and be expected to justify why they have done so. To protect covert methodology procedures should be protected from public availability. Where the interests of justice require disclosing part of a procedures document, the irrelevant content should be removed. Carelessness, in this respect by one agency, compromises the methodology for other agencies.

While space here limits the amount of discussion that can be had concerning policy and procedures the following points should be considered. First, policy and procedures should only be authored by a member trained in writing them; they are not easy to write well. Good spelling and grammar are important, and the use of unambiguous terminology is essential. That said, procedures cannot be written without the help of someone who has extensive knowledge of managing sources. The best way to write an agency's procedures is with the help of a small working group including the author, someone from management, an experienced Handler, an Investigator, an Intelligence Officer, and if possible someone from another agency who has expertise in the field. All involved need an open mind.

Second, it is the responsibility of the author to review what other agencies in the locality have in place. National, statewide, and/or regional procedures provide greater resilience for an agency than stand-alone procedures. These will always be the preferred option. The sharing of knowledge and good practice between agencies means that the procedures are much more likely to stand up to outside scrutiny than something that is limited to one agency. If these are not available, then it becomes much more important that the author reviews as many different procedures as possible. At some later stage, the agency may have to defend why it adopted a certain procedure. Evidence of due diligence goes a long way in explaining decisions.

Third, procedures should not make the job more difficult to do. Whether we think it is right or wrong, the reality is that badly written procedures encourage rule-breaking. While in and of itself rule-breaking is bad, it is also the pathway to higher levels of corruption. Inevitably good procedures require officers to be more diligent in what they do. They remove the option for shortcuts.

Fourth, there will be a lot of detail in procedures. When it comes to the depth of content, procedures should drill down into the weeds of how each task should be carried out. They should provide instruction as to what to do in about 99% of the situations that officers will encounter. Managing sources is a high-risk business and the risks come in many different ways. Procedures are an essential element in managing risk. De facto, each procedure listed, acts as a control measure for a specific risk. If an agency's procedures for managing human sources are only ten or twelve pages, more has been omitted than included, and mistakes will undoubtedly follow as a result.[2]

Fifth, the same procedures should govern all sources being managed by the agency. This includes sources

---

[2] Most good procedures are about 150 pages in length.

that are managed to support Internal Investigation departments and those reporting on terrorism/national security matters. It is accepted that in both these cases there will be a need for deviation in structures. These deviations should be minor and should be detailed in the procedures.

Sixth, procedures should not include examples. Examples illustrate a specific set of circumstances and are relevant only for that set of circumstances. However, right or wrong they may be, they are soon converted into rules and misinterpreted.

Seventh, all policies and procedures should be checked by a lawyer to ensure legislative compliance. The lawyer should pay particular regard to any civil liberty or human rights-related issues. They should also ensure that workplace safety legislation is complied with.

Finally, where a breach of policy or procedures occurs, the reason for it should be looked into. A breach of procedures does not mean the person has done something *wrong*, but it always demands an answer to the question: 'Why did you do that?' If the officer can provide a suitable explanation, then that should be enough. If they can't then it should be investigated to take disciplinary action. In reality, where procedures have been breached, the officer involved should be proactive in declaring the breach by disclosing it to a supervisor, or writing it up in a contact note. For example, where a Handler has met a source alone contrary to procedures, the contact note may read: 'Source called at 10 pm. He requested an emergency meeting. I believed there was no alternative to meeting alone. I met with him at...' With good training, Handlers are more likely to adhere to procedures and will only go outside of them when they know their actions can be justified.

Guidance

Guidance is intended to help staff carry out their work effectively, but it does not constitute rules. In essence, this book is guidance. Officers will be given guidance orally, and in written form during training. Care should be taken if an agency is issuing guidance in written format, particularly if that agency does not have good policy and comprehensive procedures. Guidance is not a substitute for either policy or procedure, and members will often justify their lack of adherence to guidance with words such as: 'It is only guidance!' Guidance infers actions are optional. With policy and procedures, there is an expectation that what is written will be followed.

Structures

We will now return to the procedures and the structures and what should be contained in them. Everything we cover from here on must be included in the procedures to say how each step will be realized within the agency. For example, where we identify a role, the functions of that role are written down in the procedures. Where we mention a record, how that record is filled in, is included in the procedures.

Dedicated Source Units

Everything advocated in this book is about professionalizing the management of sources. Sources should be managed by officers in units dedicated exclusively to that role. Here our position is clear. The evidence to support this position is overwhelming. Such measures should not be surprising as specialized units are part and parcel of most law enforcement agencies. We have teams who are dedicated to special weapons and tactics (SWAT teams); we have teams of crime scene investigators (CSI) and we have officers who exclusively perform traffic-related duties. With all these teams there is a recognition that the role requires officers to have a deep level of specialized knowledge and additional training. For some duties, it is recognized that individuals need particular aptitudes to carry out the role and that not everyone is suited. For example, the person who does not have a high level of competence with firearms is not suitable for a tactical team. Similarly, an officer who is not an effective communicator is not suitable to be a hostage negotiator, and we are highly unlikely to place someone with a rigid disposition into an undercover role. Why then do we persist in letting every officer manage human sources? Why do we think that every detective can manage sources safely and effectively?

There is a simple test if we think any officer should be allowed to manage sources. Imagine that it is your loved one who is the source, be it son, daughter, brother, lover, etc. They are passing information concerning criminal activities in your area. Would you trust their life to every officer in your agency? If your answer is yes, then you don't care much for your loved one. If your answer is no, it is a pretty safe bet that there are a limited number of officers that you think are competent enough to carry out that role. Why should other citizens not be afforded the same protection?

So before looking at why we need **_Dedicated Source Units (DSU)_** to manage all sources, let us explain exactly what we mean by the term. A Dedicated Source Unit comprises several officers whose sole function is the recruitment and management of human sources. Its members are _selected and trained_ for that role. While attached to that role they perform no other investigative function. We will revisit the structure later.

DSUs are needed to ensure that sources are managed safely and effectively and are necessary for several reasons. First, not every officer has the aptitude to manage sources. We need to pick the ones that are good at it and we need to make sure that those who do not have the aptitude to do it, are not allowed to do it.

Second, training officers to a sufficiently high standard to carry out the work effectively takes time and resources. Time and resources cost money. No agency has enough of either, to train all officers, well enough to do the role. Training requirements are discussed later. Training a limited number of officers saves a lot of money.

Third, when officers are carrying out a specific role over a period, they become much more proficient at it. Their skills are first developed and then honed. They are more productive, and they make fewer errors.

Fourth, working in small units allows for intrusive oversight of everything that is occurring. Supervisors have only one job to do which enables them to provide the maximum amount of attention to what is occurring. It keeps everyone safe and minimizes the risk of corruption.

Fifth, everything is managed much more securely, reducing the chances of the identity of the source being compromised.

Sixth, it is much easier to set up structures where there is 24/7 coverage for source contact. Each member of the Unit is competent and trained to deal with any issue that arises.

Seventh, once officers have developed a good understanding of managing human sources, they can move onto the ***proactive recruitment*** of sources, a topic discussed later. Proactive recruitment greatly enhances an agency's ability to combat organized crime and terrorism.

Source Management Team

In the system we are discussing sources are not managed by individuals, they are managed by teams working inside an identified system. A Source Management Team comprises three distinct roles: the *Handler*, the *Controller,* and the *Authorizing Officer.*

Handlers are responsible for the day-to-day management of the source. They will know the source well, regarding their capabilities as a source and their circumstances. It is the Handler that meets with the source and that is responsible for motivating that source to produce the maximum amount of quality information. It is up to the Handler to identify any risks that there may be to the safety of the source, and the integrity of the information obtained. The Handler is responsible for ensuring that the majority of records are completed. Generally speaking, a Handler can manage up to a maximum of ten sources at any one time. However, if any of them are particularly active this number will be reduced. When considering this number, it must be remembered that co-handling a source counts the same. It is the total number of sources that the Handler is involved with.

Controllers are responsible for overseeing the management of the source. They must always be at least one rank above the Handlers. They are there to ensure that the Handlers are functioning properly and to ensure that the management of the source is done ethically and legally. Controllers should be intrusive in their supervision. They should know everything that is going on with each source they are responsible for. They will meet with each source as a matter of routine, normally at the commencement of the relationship and on occasions thereafter. They should not become the 'third Handler'. They must be careful that there is separation kept between them and the source. The source should be aware that they are talking to 'the boss'. The Controller checks all paperwork submitted by the Handlers. The Controller is responsible for identifying all tasks that are to be given to a source. If someone in the agency wants the source to be tasked to gather information in support of an investigation, the Controller decides if and how it should be done. The Controller is also responsible for approving the payment of any expenses to a source up to a designated limit. Where there is an issue with any source it is the Controller's responsibility to notify the Authorizing Officer. The maximum number of sources that a Controller can supervise at any one time is twenty. However, if any of the sources are particularly active this number will be reduced. Furthermore, the Controller cannot be expected to be on call 24/7. There must be a Deputy Controller who can help during periods of leave or sickness.

The Authorizing Officer is responsible for authorizing all sources on behalf of the agency, save for when there is an exceptional risk in managing a particular source. In deciding to authorize a source the Authorizing Officer must look across the whole source program and decide if there are sufficient resources to manage all the sources that are registered. If they are at their limit registering another source may be a foolish option. The Authorizing Officer is also responsible for deciding any financial remuneration that is to be paid to a source regularly. (Finances are discussed in Chapter 8.) There is no requirement for the Authorizing Officer to be aware of the daily activities of any source. Only when there are problems that require their intervention, should they become involved. The maximum number of sources that an Authorizing Officer can be responsible for is fifty. This assumes that it is their only job within the agency. Where sources become involved in more complex operations, much of the Authorizing Officer's time will be taken up making strategic decisions in liaison with other officers such as Investigators and other specialized departments. Here again, there needs to be a Deputy Authorizing Officer that can cover for periods of leave, and if the workload becomes excessive.

Twenty years into the 21st Century it seems incredible that this next fact needs to be pointed out. When meeting with a source, at least one of the Handler's must be the same gender as the source. Without going into a whole discussion about the meaning of the word gender, let us just keep this simple. If the source defines themselves as a female there must be a female officer present. If the source defines themselves as male there must be a male officer present. Entering into a sexual relationship with a source is one of the most prevalent forms of corruption present in policing. Furthermore, allegations of inappropriate behavior are quite easy to make. Handlers are much more likely to be believed if there is someone of the same gender as the source, present at all times. In short, we need to make sure that the Dedicated Source Unit has both male and female officers.

In a similar vein, the more diverse the make-up of a Unit is the more options that are created for that team. This is most relevant where an agency is working in an area where the community is made up of a diverse population and/or where different languages are spoken, by sizeable sections of the community

Each trained Handler and Controller should be allocated an operational code number on their appointment to a Dedicated Source Unit. This number stays with them throughout their career and is used exclusively on all source records. Handlers and Controllers should not put their names on any source document. This affords better protection to the source and the officer.

For each source, there is a Source Management Team (referred to throughout as the Team). The team members for one source will also be team members for other sources. The structure of a source management team is outlined in Figure 2.2

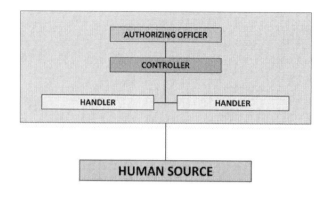

Figure 2.2 A Source Management Team

Returning to the Dedicated Source Units we can see how they will operate in the management of several sources.

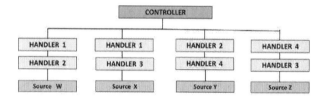

Figure 2.3 A Dedicated Source Unit

As we can see in this example, the Controller is responsible for four Handlers who are at the minute manging four sources. Obviously, this DSU can manage more sources. Furthermore, there is no necessity for the Authorizing Officer to be co-located with the Dedicated Source Unit. In larger agencies, this basic model is expanded to meet the needs of the agency.

Figure 2.4 Dedicated Source Units

Figure 2.4 illustrates how several DSUs work under the supervision of a solitary Authorizing Officer. However, we should also recognize the fact that if these three units are working to full capacity, the Authorizing Officer may be exceeding their capacity. A judgment call will have to be made to see if there is a requirement for an additional Authorizing Officer. It may be that the Deputy Authorizing Officer has to take full charge of a limited number of cases.

When it comes to the management of sources here is an additional role that is needed. This is the role of **Senior Responsible Officer**. The senior responsible officer will be the Head of the Agency in smaller agencies, and in others maybe the Deputy Head or similar: think Deputy Chief or Assistant Commissioner. Their role is to make all strategic decisions about source management. This will include approving the policy and procedures and ensuring there is adequate staff to carry out the roles. They will also be responsible for ensuring that there is sufficient budget to make payments to sources. Also, they will make any decision where there is a significant risk to the agency, and they will *approve* any source that the

Authorizing Officer deems High-Risk. The Authorizing Officer normally has more detailed knowledge of source management and more experience of the issues. Theirs is a position of expertise. However, it is the responsibility of the Senior Responsible Officer to manage the strategic risk to the organization. Therefore, their *approval* must be given, or a high-risk source cannot be registered. In effect, the Authorizing Officer is saying 'We can manage this source, provided you accept the level of risk to the agency'. (More on this later.) Where an agency gets bigger, the structures need to expand accordingly. For example, a large agency may cover an area with a large urban center and six districts. (See Figure 2.5.)

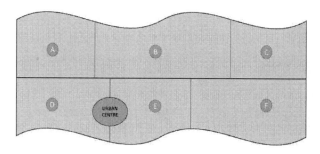

Figure 2.5 A Large Area of Responsibility

As the size of the agency increases, with it comes increased capacity to deal with a greater number of crimes and higher-level criminality. In our example above, we may find that in the Urban Centre not only is there ordinary street-level crime but there is also organized crime and a threat from extremist activity/terrorism. If this is the case the agency is going to need a total of nine Dedicated Source Units and three Authorizing Officers will be required - One to cover districts A, B, and C, one to cover D, E and F, and one to cover the three units in the Urban Centre.

As the capacity of the agency increases another role becomes increasingly important, that of **Source Administrator.** Where an agency has a large number of sources, there needs to be a central point where the true identities of sources can be held, together with their enhanced profiles (See Chapter 3). Before a Handler registers a source, they should check with the Source Administrator to see if that source is, or has been, previously registered. This deconfliction ensures that two separate units are not managing the same source, or that they end up manging a source who was previously declared as being dangerous. The Source Administrator is also the place where an Investigator can request if the agency has any source that can help with their investigation. The Source Administrator can search the records to see if any source meets those criteria and if they do notify the relevant Controller of the request.

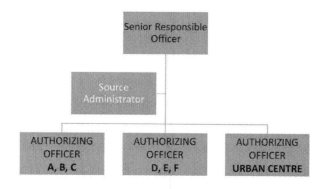

Figure 2.6 Large Agency Structures

Numbers

As will have been seen what we are discussing here requires the agency to have a prerequisite number of officers to manage sources in this way. While this may work in many jurisdictions it creates difficulties for somewhere there are a large number of very small agencies, most noticeably the USA. Unfortunately, the risks for a small agency are no different from those faced by a large agency, and therefore everything we are suggesting here as appropriate control measures for those risks, remains the same. It helps to establish a baseline about the number of sources that an agency can safely manage. The circumstances vary from agency to agency and there are some variables that we need to take cognizance of in arriving at a baseline figure. First of all, is the geographical area that the agency covers. Some law enforcement agencies cover huge sparsely populated areas while others cover densely populated areas. The area size and population density have to be factored in. Also, the nature and level of criminality being investigated will play a part. Furthermore, there may be some different agencies working against the same criminals, a problem we will discuss later. While there may be adjustments that have to be made after taking all these factors into account a baseline figure for the number of sources that an agency can manage at any one time can be worked out using the following formula:

$$Number\ of\ sources = \frac{\text{Number of officers}}{30}$$

The number thirty is derived from considering the number of manhours that are required for a source meeting (4 hours per officer per meeting) the number of hours that need to be spent in recruiting a source, and the number of hours in support functions such as supervision and utilizing the product. While some may dispute the results that they obtain from this formula, increasing the number of sources derived from it can only be achieved by cutting corners and exposing the agency to greater risks. If the law enforcement agency has no uniform or patrol functions, their function being exclusively the investigation of crime then, they will be able to manage more sources.

As an example, if we are using this formula, we can see that if an agency has 300 staff, they can safely manage 10 sources at any one time. While this may not make pleasant reading for small agencies, if it is thought through properly, it will be obvious that the sources the agency currently has, are not being used properly. Of course, this assumes that there is sufficient knowledge within the agency to properly identify the risks involved. Unfortunately, if they continue managing sources and something goes wrong, there will be plenty of lawyers lining up to point out exactly where they went wrong.

The simple solution to this problem is that of inter-agency working. Memorandums of understanding are agreed and some officers from different agencies establish a Dedicated Source Unit to manage sources for all the partner agencies. There are operational difficulties in this and generally speaking one agency will have to take the lead, with the others sharing the cost. All officers in the DSU must work to the same procedures and utilize the same records.

Where an officer from a small agency encounters a person, who is in a position to provide valuable information and is willing to do so, there are two options. The first option is that the officer takes the information on a one-time basis. No relationship is established, and the person is considered to fall into the category of Member of the Public (MoP) as discussed in Chapter 1. The second option is for the officer to introduce the person member of a Dedicated Source Unit in a larger neighboring agency. Agreements should be put in place to ensure that the initiating agency continues to obtain the benefit from any intelligence gained through that source. Such arrangements rely on good structures and professional courtesy.

Always two

There must always be at least two Handlers responsible for the management of a source. With sources who are extremely active, and an additional Handler may be needed to cope with the workload. It is the responsibility of these Handlers to manage the source daily, address their needs, and obtain the information that the source is expected to provide. Sources should never be managed by just one officer. It is an urban myth, proclaimed mainly by insecure officers that 'the source will only talk to me'. It is a similar mindset as is present when we hear 'He is my source.' Both these remarks are an indication that the Handler has lost their objectivity.

Two Handlers must always be present at all meetings with the source. This is not negotiable. There are many reasons. First, officer safety. Meeting sources is physically dangerous. If only one officer is present, they are in much greater danger. Second, source safety. The source is in danger during meetings. There is a much better chance of keeping them safe if there are two sets of eyes watching. Third, as we will discuss in detail later, debriefing a source is complex. Two brains are much better than one, when it comes to thinking of everything that is needed. Fourth, there is much less chance of an inappropriate relationship developing between a Handler and the source if there are two Handlers present. In source management, there is always the risk of a Handler losing objectivity and becoming involved in a personal relationship with the source. This may involve the Handler providing favors

57

for the source or the source providing favors for the Handler. Fifth, a source may make allegations that a Handler did something wrong or did not do something they should have done. Having two officers present makes it a lot easier to refute such allegations. Sixth, there is a real risk that the motives of the source are wholly corrupt. They are there just to use the Handler. The source never has the intention to form a mutually beneficial relationship. Unfortunately, with some officers, their egos will not even permit them to acknowledge that they may have been taken in. However, ask any experienced Handler who has been at it a while, and they will tell you, not only when they were taken in, but they will also be able to break it down into the many subtle ways that were used to sucker them. We all like to think we are smarter than everyone else in the room and the smartest guy[3] in the room lets us continue to believe. There must <u>always</u> be two Handlers present with a source.

Analysts

Where staffing levels permit, there is considerable benefit in having trained analysts intrinsically involved in source management. Larger agencies, where Dedicated Source Units have a proactive capacity, will benefit greatly from having an analyst in each team or shared between two or three teams, depending on

---

[3] Actually, the smartest person in the room is more likely to be a woman, because us guys are too busy telling each other how amazing we are.

58

workload. There is much that an analyst can add to source management including identifying tasking opportunities for the source through social network analysis. They can prepare timelines based on what the source has declared has happened and compare these with other information that is at hand, to either verify what the source has said or identify discrepancies. Furthermore, the ability of an analyst to present data in different formats can help the source management team identify any problems that are occurring rather than trying to keep dates and events in their working memory. A chart showing significant events in the source relationship such as the date of recruitment, a change in Handler, a major personal crisis, etc, make it easy for a Controller to keep on top of things. As they will be managing up to twenty different sources at any one time, it is easy to see how they would decide about one source while basing it on the history of another. Collating performance indicators is another valuable function as is preparing comparisons between information submitted and intelligence subsequently action by *intelligence customers*.

Analysts are trained to draw conclusions based on limited information. This can be very useful at the beginning of a source relationship where it is all but impossible to decide if the source is providing accurate information and to the extent that should lie within that source's knowledge. In the early stages, the evidence is likely to be very fuzzy indeed, yet it is at this time that everyone involved is asking: 'Is this guy for real, or is he just yanking our chain?'

Analysts should also be used to identify potential tasks for the source. By plotting out the various entities to which the source has access, opportunities may be presented either for the greater reporting by the source on existing relationships, or the potential for the source to develop new relationships where further information can be gathered. For example, the source may have reported once on person 'Z' but be continually reporting on W, X, and Y. If there is a legitimate reason for the source to contact Z, this potentially opens up another avenue of reporting. Handlers often miss these opportunities because they are focussed on managing the relationship and on the information that is coming to them, without seeking more out.

Psychologists

Where possible, it is beneficial if the agency has an in-house psychologist, who is cleared to discuss matters about the management of sources. Handling sources can cause problems for an officer's mental health. If they do not have access to a mental health professional with whom they are allowed to discuss these issues, there is a real chance that the problems will fester inside. In addition, sources passing information do so at significant risk to both their physical wellbeing and are subject to noteworthy psychological pressure (Billingsley, 2009). It is far from unusual that a source reacts excessively and dangerously to that pressure. Where there are indications of serious mental health problems with a source it may be appropriate for the

60

psychologist to meet with the source. However, there need to be truly clear structures in place as there may be a conflict for the psychologist concerning who their 'client' is – the source or the agency. Where mental health issues create ethical conflicts, the psychologist should be included in the Strategic Advisory Group meeting (see below).

Having said that, there is no benefit in having every source meet with a psychologist. Many sources will come from dysfunctional backgrounds and may well have underlying mental health conditions that while present, do not inhibit their day-to-day functioning. If a psychologist begins to expose such issues, ethically, the agency is committing to fix them. We can't lift the rug and leave it for someone else to fix what we have exposed. For sources, meeting with a psychologist should be the exception rather than the rule. For Handler's, there is a strong case for them to speak with a psychologist on an annual basis for the Handler's well-being.

Investigator

In this context, an Investigator is a person in charge of any investigation, to which the source is contributing information. The Investigator may on occasions know that there is a human source providing information. For the most part, there is no requirement for them to know the identity of the source. However, where the source is particularly close to the investigation, of necessity the Investigator will need to know the source's identity, so that they are not compromised as a result of the investigation.

Strategic management

When a source is first recruited, the source management team should agree short, medium, and long-term goals for the source. Three, six, and twelve-month periods are realistic for short, medium, and long-term. These goals should be agreed after the Handlers have had the opportunity to identify the access the source has to target groups and the source's capabilities concerning their role as a source. The Handlers and the Controller should meet regularly to discuss if, and to what extent these goals are being met.

Strategic Advisory Group

There can be many potentially difficult decisions to be made with the management of a human source. These will include decisions concerning the ethics of managing a particular source, decisions about terminating a source, and the operational deployment of a source. There may be Senior Responsible Officers who feel that because they have the right to make that decision, that this alone qualifies them to make the decision. This is hubris talking. To help ensure that the best decisions are made, it is recommended that the Senior Responsible Officer brings together and several experts that can provide input to aid in the decision making. Strategic Advisory Groups (SAG) are made up of different people depending upon the question at hand. Generally speaking, they will always involve the Senior Responsible Officer, the Authorizing Officer, the Controller or a Handler, and the agency lawyer. The idea is to bring balance to the decision making. If the question at hand is an ethical one, aside from the fact that the majority of those involved should be trained in ethical decision making, it is useful to have someone designated to hold to the 'highest ethical ground' perspective. It is highly likely that the 'ends justify the means' perspective will be represented already by the majority in the room. (More on ethics in Chapter 8.)

When a source is to be involved in an operational deployment such as assisting in an undercover operation, participating in a crime, or assisting in a surveillance operation then the representation of all aspects of the operation must be covered. In addition to those mentioned above, the group must include the Investigator who will be responsible for identifying issues affecting the investigation including the potential *disclosure* in court of the source's role. Others attending may include the officer in charge of any surveillance team and/or the officer in charge of any undercover operative.

Minutes should be prepared for any meeting of a Strategic Advisory Group and included in or attached to the decision log for the source. Members of a SAG are there in an advisory capacity. While the views of each member should be noted, any decision taken rests solely with the Senior Responsible Officer.

Human rights and civil liberties

The reason law enforcement exists is to protect human rights and civil liberties. In managing human sources there is the potential for law enforcement to engage with human rights and standards, and civil liberty expectations. These issues can stray into areas of quite complex law. That said, there are a few basic principles that if understood, mean that the actions of the source are compliant with these standards. First, is the *'right to life'*. Law enforcement agencies are obligated to protect life. This includes the life of a source. If an agency does not take measures that are reasonably practical to protect the life of the source, they are likely to be breaching the source's human rights. For example, sending officers to meet with a source, who are not trained in fieldcraft, puts the source's life in danger (and the lives of officers – two breaches for the price of one!) Second, people have a *'right to privacy'*. Law enforcement cannot 'spy' on people without justification. This includes asking a source to spy for the agency. If a source is collecting information about a person, the agency must have justified in writing, why they are doing it. If a source is watching who comes and goes from a neighbor's house, they are engaging that person's right to privacy. This action must be justified. Third, is the *'right to a fair trial'*. When using a source to aid in investigations, there is the potential to create a situation where there is a question mark over whether or not the involvement of the source brings into doubt the guilt of the defendant. Fair trial concerns often raise their head with issues of disclosure.

All law enforcement agencies should conduct their activities with respect for human rights and civil liberties. Managing sources is an area where interpretations of the relevant case law are often nuanced. Specialized legal advice may be needed but unfortunately, many prosecutors do not have the depth of knowledge required. Agencies can often pre-empt problems if they have a Handler within the agency who has the relevant expert knowledge.

Source 'agreements'

Many agencies like a source to sign some form of agreement or 'terms and conditions' on commencing their role as a source. While it is always beneficial to explain to a source what they can and cannot do, and the reasons for these rules, getting them to sign some sort of agreement, in most cases serves only as a comfort blanket for the ill-informed. Rarely will such agreements have any legal standing and then, only if they have been made with a lawyer present to represent the source. However, having a lawyer present means there is someone else who knows the person is a source and someone else that has to be trusted not to disclose the role of the source accidentally or deliberately.

Before delving into a legislative discussion about some of the issues that may invalidate any such agreement, try and imagine the circumstances where law enforcement might rely on this document as evidence. The first one that comes to mind is that the agency wants to show that the source did not have an exemption from breaking a law. This is reasonable except that many times the agency will be aware the source is breaking the law and turn a blind eye to it. For example, the source who is a drug dealer is asked to sign an agreement that they will not break the law. What the agency wants here is to be able to say: 'We told him not to do it and looked they signed here.' At the same time, the source was being repeatedly tasked to associate with other drug dealers, and the contact notes and information submissions make it obvious he is involved in criminality. Second, perhaps the source has been compromised and the agency wants to say it was the fault of the source. An agreement is unlikely to support this, especially if the Handlers were untrained and failed to provide the source with any training.

The third case may be where a source has made a deal that they will give a certain amount or type of information to have a reduced sentence or charges dropped. While an agreement like this may have some legal weight, it has extremely limited utility from an information collection perspective. The source will provide the very least they must to fulfill their agreement. More often than not, they will give up two or three low-level criminals whose arrest has no impact on the problem. Many criminals are quite happy to give up the small fry when it comes to protecting themselves. In other cases, such agreements are likely to lead to allegations of entrapment.

Looking at these agreements from a legal perspective their worth becomes even more questionable. First, it is likely to be argued that the agreement is unconscionable in law. This term can be explained by the use of less legalistic language. An unconscionable agreement is one such as 'no man in his senses and not under delusion would make on the one hand, and as no honest and fair man would accept on the other'. Typical source agreements are so one-sided that no one could argue that the source was treated as an equal. Where in the agreement does it specify what financial rewards the source can expect or what the agency undertakes to provide in terms of support?

Second, many of these agreements commence with words like 'I consent...' Is this informed consent? What is the source consenting to? What does it mean to be a human source? When exploring this issue, we need to draw on all the case law about informed consent and there is a lot to it. For example, has the advantages and disadvantages of what they are doing been fully explained to the source? Have they been given a full breakdown of the proposed activity, including the purpose, type, methods, and likely duration of it? This is rarely the case.

Third, when we talk about consent, if the circumstances change is the consent still valid, or is a new agreement needed? How often do Handlers hear sources say: 'I didn't sign up for this.' Whatever the new 'this' is that is being proposed. Being a source is not a fixed situation. It is constantly changing and evolving. Where in these agreements does it say how a source can withdraw consent. This is a legal entitlement with contracts, in many jurisdictions.

Fourth, has the source the knowledge and intellectual ability to fully appreciate what they are agreeing to and what the future consequences of their signature may be?

Fifth, there is a huge imbalance of power in the relationship, and law enforcement often explicitly threaten sources with long terms of imprisonment unless they become sources. This falls into the realm of procedural unconscionability, where one party to an agreement has no real choice.

Finally, there is no potential redress for the source. If the agency fails to fulfill its commitments, the source is all but powerless to do anything. Even if they could afford to take a lawsuit, in doing so they automatically compromise their identity and their safety.

If an agency wants to use agreements, the only immediate issue is the fact that they create conflict with the source in getting them to sign. And if there is no conflict, it is a strong indicator that the source has absolutely no intention of abiding by it. One of the reasons that conflict is likely to arise is based on a psychological theory known as cognitive dissonance (Festinger, 1957) though there are many other aspects at play including ego defense mechanisms. Cognitive dissonance can be explained thus: No one wants to be seen as a rat! Or, in a deeper way thus: Being a human source often involves the betrayal of a person's tribe, friends, and family. This idea is contrary to many of our basic belonging and safety needs. When a person does this, then their behavior creates internal conflict with their values. This state is called cognitive dissonance. It can be very unpleasant for a person. Many of us know this feeling as guilt. And we all know how much we want to get rid of that feeling. What happens in the source relationship is that the source projects the guilt onto the Handler and a conflict ensues. There are sufficient conflicts in a source relationship without wilfully creating them, but if the agency is happy with this, then that is probably the extent of the harm initially. However, if the agency hopes to rely on such an agreement in the event of something serious occurring, then the agreement will be about as much use as a comfort blanket is to a child when the real bogey man comes to call.

High-risk and dangerous sources, and intelligence nuisances

There is danger in managing any source. The Handler is placed in physical risk every time they meet with a source. The degree of this risk depends on the context in which they are meeting and the nature of the source they are meeting. While these risks can be mitigated through good fieldcraft, the danger can never be totally removed. There is a danger that the source will tell lies, distorting what is already in the agency's intelligence system and or damaging an investigation. All risks can be managed. However, an assessment needs to be carried out to see if the potential benefits to be gained outweigh the cost of managing the risk. There are several sorts of individual that will require additional consideration before being registered.

The first of these is what we will refer to as ***High-Risk*** sources. A high-risk source is a source who because of their previous history, the extent of their ongoing connection with criminality, or their social position or background, have been deemed by the Authorizing Officer as requiring additional control measures for them to be managed safely. We will now examine why some people are likely to be designated High-Risk.

The first of these is where a person has an extensive criminal history that would raise public concern if they were being managed by the agency. The Senior Responsible Officer will normally create a list of offenses which if the person has been convicted of them or is suspected of them, automatically makes them a High-Risk source. This list is likely to include things like murder and serious sexual assaults, especially against children. This list should be limited to crimes where the level of public concern evokes the greatest emotional response. The risk involved is potential damage to the agency's reputation if it is discovered.

The second sort of High-Risk source is one where the source is heavily connected to ongoing criminality or is committing crimes. Someone who is a member of an organized crime gang is likely to be caught up in ongoing criminality. Individuals like this are often not fully committed to their role as a source, and attempt to keep a foot in both camps. They need to be managed with the greatest rigor by the most experienced of Handlers. Processes need to be in place to ensure that there is no 'turning a blind eye' to their criminality. The agency takes its information with one hand and investigates their criminality with the other.

In a similar vein is the source who is reporting on terrorism or national security matters. Here there are substantial physical risks to both the Handlers and the source. In addition, in most countries, being a member of a terrorist organization is a criminal offense. De facto, the source continues to commit that offense through the entirety of their relationship with the agency.

The third type of person that is likely to be deemed High-Risk is someone whose occupation or social status adds additional complications. These people will include journalists, lawyers, clergy, or medical professionals. With all these people there is an expectation that they will come in contact with some information where others have a high expectation of confidentiality. Each of these cases must be examined on the circumstances they present. However, there must also be discernment. Just because someone writes a few blogs does not make them a journalist, nor is everyone who preaches clergy. To see if they fall into the category it is useful to look for some formal type of accreditation. While many of these people will willing pass information to the police, they may be bound by professional guidelines such as doctor/patient privilege. Nevertheless, there are also cases where such people are similarly bound to pass certain information to police. The key element here is a detailed examination of what is proposed and the continuous monitoring of the relationship.

High-Risk sources should only be managed where there is a significant benefit to be gained and no practical alternatives exist. The authorization for a High-Risk source must be approved by the Senior Responsible Officer. The High-Risk source should only be managed if at least one of the Handlers is deemed experienced (see training later). The underlying principle with High-Risk sources is that the agency will manage them but will put in place additional control measures to mitigate the additional risk.

Where a source has wilfully or negligently exposed the agency to additional risk, the Authorizing Officer should designate that source as *'Dangerous'* and cease all further interaction with them. Their source file should be labeled accordingly, the understanding being that unless the most extreme of circumstances exist, that person will never be managed as a source. People that are likely to be labeled as dangerous are those who have been involved in corrupting or attempting to corrupt an officer, those having made unfounded allegations against a member of the Source Management Team, and those who continually and willfully engaged in deceit. Just because a source has told a few lies does not make them a Dangerous source, nor should it, as a matter of course, preclude them from being a source.[4] With Dangerous sources, there is a threshold that has been surpassed.

---

[4] First, we all lie. Second, many times when a source lies it's because they don't feel safe enough to tell the truth.

Another sort of person that Handlers are likely to encounter is the ***Intelligence Nuisance.*** An Intelligence Nuisance is a person who repeatedly provides information to law enforcement that while outwardly appearing to be credible, is at the core false. This type of person interweaves truths and half-truths with fabrications and can easily mislead the inexperienced officer. For example, they may talk about a well-known major criminal, (truth) who they know is about to bring in drugs (half-truth - the criminal is always bringing in drugs but the source has no idea when) and they are sure the criminal will tell them the whole story soon (complete fabrication). Not only do these people waste a considerable amount of time and effort, but when an officer fails to accurately evaluate the information and enters it into the intelligence system, this bad intelligence can also corrupt any existing intelligence it touches. Furthermore, these individuals oftcn have mental health issues. They may be the typical Walter Mitty. If an agency manages this person as a source, it may well put that person's life in danger. These people should be designated accordingly, and warning placed on their file.

Intelligence-led policing (ILP)

While the reactive, investigative side to law enforcement remains a core part of modern-day policing, in more recent years there has been a shift in the paradigm away from the reactive approach and towards a proactive approach. This is dominated by the concept of Intelligence-Led Policing (ILP) in all its various forms. The thrust of Intelligence-Led Policing is about using the limited resources that law enforcement has, in more effective ways. There are three key aspects to ILP. First, is maximizing the amount of information available to the police including crime statistics, information from investigation, and through 'covert' information-gathering methods. Covert methods include the use of human sources, surveillance, the interception of communications, and undercover operations. The second aspect is the processing of that information into intelligence. Third, is the use of that intelligence to prevent crime and to target offenders. An obvious assumption that can be made is that, if Intelligence-Led Policing is to realize its full potential, then it is critical to obtain the maximum amount of good quality intelligence.

If the right sources are recruited, and managed effectively, against agreed objectives, the amount of information they will produce is likely to surpass what any agency can deal with. Regarding sources, the most important aspect of ILP is the biannual supply of intelligence requirements. At the start of a year, the Authorizing Officer should be told what the intelligence needs of the agency are. Sources should then be managed to address those needs. Halfway through the year, these requirements should be reviewed to ensure the agency's strategy is working. It is unrealistic to change the general taskings of a source more often than every six months. It takes a source time to establish the relationships where they can obtain the desired information in any quantity.

Understanding intelligence

Source management does not operate in a vacuum. Many law enforcement activities interlink with it, including investigation, undercover operations, and surveillance. Central to all of these is the management of intelligence. As we highlighted in Chapter 1 we manage sources to collect information and we turn this information into intelligence. That intelligence is then used to inform other aspects of law enforcement. Those involved in source management need to have a good understanding of how an intelligence management system should work, and how the management of sources connects with that system. We will begin with a brief overview of how an agency can manage intelligence, to ensure that what is needed gets to the right place.

All information is submitted in a standard format (an information submission) to a centralized Intelligence Unit. In the Intelligence Unit, the information is analyzed, evaluated, and anonymized. An intelligence report is created and stored in the Intelligence Repository[5], where it can be accessed at any time in the future, by those cleared to see it. The Intelligence Unit also disseminates this intelligence to whomever they deem most appropriate to act upon it. The recipient acts upon it and returns the results to the Intelligence

---

[5] Intelligence repository - An intelligence repository is a central storage point for all intelligence products. Imagine a big filing cabinet but in a computer.

Unit, who in turn, informs the originator of the information.

Figure 2.8 illustrates an intelligence management system. On the left lists how information can be collected. It is then passed to the Intelligence Unit who process it, store it and if appropriate disseminate it for action. All information that is collected for intelligence purposes must go to the Intelligence Unit *before* it can be used, save for where there is an imminent threat to life. A source does not phone in a piece of information so the Investigator can rush out and kick in a door without the information first being processed. The process is the same when information comes from any of the other origins shown in Figure 2.8.

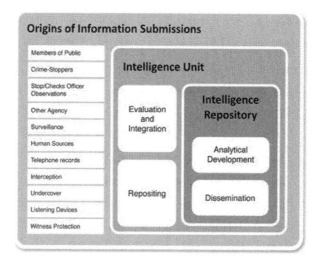

Figure 2.8 An Intelligence Management System

An example of what is involved is given to illustrate what happens when a source provides information.

A source who has previously provided accurate information says there are presently large quantities of illicit drugs in the 5th Avenue, Blacktown, home of Tony Christie. The source was told this by Christie. The Handler submits this to the Intelligence Unit. The Intelligence Unit identifies previous recent reporting on Tony Christie that he is a major drug dealer. They know he lives in a house at 63, 5th Avenue, Blacktown. The Intelligence Unit creates an intelligence report on drug possession and lodges it in the Intelligence Repository. They then disseminate this intelligence report, together with the previous reporting, for action to a Narcotics Unit. The Narcotics Unit uses the intelligence reports, which are independently assessed by the Intelligence Unit as containing reliable intelligence, to obtain a warrant. They search the house and notify the Intelligence Unit of the result. In turn, the Intelligence Unit notify the Controller.

There are several advantages to the process like this. First, there is a distance between the search and the source. This firewall affords a better chance of the source's identity not being disclosed. Second, the intelligence provided to the judge has been verified as being reliable, independently of the investigation by the Intelligence Unit. Their assessment of each intelligence report is contained in the evaluation code on the document. (More on this in Chapter 6.) Independent evaluation of the source and intelligence protects civil liberties and ensures human rights compliance. Third, it protects the Investigator for allegations that they made up the intelligence.

Strategic and tactical intelligence

The source will be tasked to collect both *strategic* and *tactical* intelligence. The separation between these two types of intelligence comes primarily from how any piece of intelligence is used or is likely to be used, i.e. its intended purpose. Strategic intelligence focuses on the structure of organized crime, including terrorism, patterns in on-going criminal activity, and the threat posed by emerging criminal trends. It tells senior management what is happening and what is likely to happen in the future concerning criminality. Strategic intelligence enables senior management to effectively deploy resources against currently identified threats/problems and emerging problems and to develop control strategies. Tactical intelligence is intelligence regarding a specific criminal activity that can be used to further a criminal investigation, plan tactical operations, and provide for public safety at specific events.

Something may be of interest or use at a strategic level, may be of limited interest or use, to those at a tactical level, and vice versa. Handlers need to know the difference and they need to know which type of intelligence the source is expected to provide. Deploying a source in one way may negate an opportunity to collect information that will be used for the type of intelligence that is desired. There is a tendency to focus on tactical intelligence because it is likely to bring instantaneous results. Typical examples of what is lost when Handlers do not seek out strategic intelligence include, the structures of criminal gangs, the internal politics of these gangs, and their long-term strategies. Sources will probably have a limited understanding of why such material would be of use to law enforcement and therefore not even think to mention what they know in this regard.

Intelligence Unit responsibilities

The Intelligence Unit has several responsibilities with sources. First, is the processing of information. Second, they should provide feedback to the Controller about the quality of that information identifying inaccuracies or discrepancies with other reporting. Third, they should also provide the Controller with additional taskings for the source regarding specific intelligence that is needed. For example, Can the source find out where Ben Thomas is currently living? Does the source know anyone who goes by the nickname 'Bunk'? These queries can be raised within the Intelligence Unit or generated externally. They ensure that the agency gains the maximum benefit from the source.

Fourth, as the recipient of all the information that comes from Members of the Public (MoPs), the Unit will know the name of the person who originated the information. The Unit should liaise with a Controller to identify any MoP whose status may be drifting into one of being a human source and to assess if that person should be registered as a human source. This prevents people from being run 'off the books' by officers and also serve to talent-spot individuals who may make a good source.

Fifth, inevitably those working in the Intelligence Unit may become aware of the identity of a source. The upside of this is that they can forewarn a Controller where there is adverse reporting on a source, allowing the Controller to revisit the source's risk assessment.

Pre-authorization checks

Before any source is authorized to become a source for the agency, a comprehensive check must be carried out concerning any previous convictions they have and any intelligence that is held on them. Things like domestic violence databases and sex offender databases should also be checked. These are needed so that the Authorizing Officer has a clear picture of who they are authorizing to become a source. Ideally, the Handler should be able to carry out such checks without the need to highlight to anyone that the individual concerned is being considered for registration as a source.

Intelligence customers

Sources can provide many different types of information that can support a whole range of different policing functions. For the maximum benefit to be obtained the first thing that is required is professional Handlers that have the knowledge and experience to be able to recognize opportunities where the source can help. Moreover, those involved in Dedicate Source Units have to promote the service they can provide across the agency through briefings and training sessions. Most officers have no real understanding as to what sources can do, viewing them with deep suspicion and totally underestimating the extent to which a good source can help them. People will often spend weeks looking for a piece of information that a Handler could find out with a phone call. There must also be mechanisms within an agency for centralized tasking of sources. Moreover, the Dedicated Source Unit should have an 'open door' mindset, encouraging other officers to visit and ask for help.

Intelligence entities

Handlers have to be able to write up the information they get from sources. To do this well they have to be aware of what is expected by Intelligence Officers concerning detail. Furthermore, in law enforcement, there is an expectation that much of what is submitted by a Handler will be acted upon. Accurate details are required. One aspect of intelligence that Handlers are often unfamiliar with is the concept of *entities*.

Entities are a core part of any intelligence system. An entity is defined as: 'a unique element that when inputted into the intelligence repository falls within an identified category of, person, geographic location or item.' (Buckley, 2016) In short, an entity is a uniquely identified person, place, or thing. Entities will always fall within one of a limited number of specified categories, as identified by the agency's intelligence management procedures. The following are the most frequently used categories:

Persons. A person entity will be built upon the person's name and while this may appear simple at first glance, there is more to it than initially obvious. Name entities include nicknames, aliases, and the spelling of ethnically diverse names. Other data likely to be found in the entity screen includes details of the person's social security number, offender reference number, passport details, driving license, etc.

Geographic locations. Geographic locations will include housing and commercial premises, streets, towns, etc. Data fields for geographic locations are likely to include the official address, zip codes/postcodes, type of structure, the use to which it is put, the number of stories, access and egress details, ownership and occupancy details, and contact details for both. Where possible, all geographic locations should be geo-coded before entry into the repository.

Article. An article can be anything whether tangible or not. It is for the officer creating the entity to decide as to what should fall into this category or what might be better placed in one of the other categories. Items are likely to include such things as weapons, narcotics, and monetary instruments. When recording such entities, the more comprehensive the details inputted the greater benefit will be had in the longer term.

Means of Transport. This type of entity will include all the obvious means of transport including cars, buses, aircraft, trains, and shipping. Any statutory registration numbers or names should be included where known. For example, with a ship, the name of a ship, and its place of registration.

Means of Communication. Communication was once relatively simple, there were letters, telegrams, telephones, and radios and that was about it. Then technology exploded with the advent of the internet and mobile cellular phones and has continued to expand with the development of numerous apps. This will include encryption methods.

Organization. Organizations will include both criminal gangs and legitimate organizations. Where a person is associated with an organization, they should be linked to it.

Event. Events will include crimes committed and non-criminal events such as political rallies, demonstrations, and entertainment. Events may or may not be recorded as criminal occurrences for the simple reason they may never have been reported, for example, a major drug importation by a criminal gang. If such events are not recorded as intelligence, failure to find them when further intelligence is obtained can skew the interpretation of that intelligence.

When a Handler becomes familiar with the concept of entities there will likely be a rise over time, in the quantity and quality of information they are providing. This is because the Handler will begin to seek more detail from the source and in turn, the source will learn that greater detail is required.

Training

Training officers on how to manage sources is essential and should be done before they start to do it. Those who think that you don't need to be trained and you can learn on the job, probably also advocate surgeons 'learning on the job'. Most of us would prefer the surgeon who has done the training before they start sticking a knife into us. If someone says managing sources can only be learned by doing it, it is obvious straight away they don't know what they are talking about. All officers involved in managing human sources need to be trained to carry out that function safely and effectively. Training reduces risks. Many avoidable mistakes occur because the officer involved is not professionally trained.

Training is expensive. Officers have to be removed from their posts and for a limited period are not productive. Many managers believe that officers can pick up what they need to know as they go along. Many senior managers believe that they never need to go to any training course because they are so smart, they already know everything they need to know. Making training mandatory for all involved raises the standards

84

across the agency and has long-term benefits regarding productivity. Training is an investment in the future. Remember, one of the key benefits of having only dedicated officers manage sources is that training only needs to be delivered to an extremely limited number of officers.

In designing source management training, we have to be realistic about what is necessary for an officer to have before they carry out the role. Training must provide sufficient knowledge for the officer to do the job *competently*. Training courses must recognize that any agency has only a limited number of hours in which to deliver new knowledge. For example, a professor may say many different theories of motivation should be covered so we can better motivate the source, but they have had a lifetime to study it, and a semester to share it with their students. In police training, we may have four hours to cover this topic.

We will begin by discussing what must be taught for the agency to know that they have taken measures that were *reasonably practical* to ensure the safety of all involved. We will consider different levels of training, so that training is constructed to provide the necessary knowledge for the function the person is undertaking, and we will provide suggestions for developmental training. Several basic principles apply across the board. First, all training should be intended to make the officer competent for their role. Competence indicates that an officer has sufficient *knowledge* and *skills* that enable them to act in a wide variety of situations which they are likely to encounter. Training

85

is about providing the knowledge and then checking that the person has the skill to utilize that knowledge. If an officer cannot demonstrate they can perform the tasks involved, they should not be allowed to handle sources. Some source training will be pass or fail.

Second, training should be delivered against an agreed set of standards. There will be different standards for different ranks. The more agencies that have agreed to the standards the more resilient they will be. For example, in the USA if all the law enforcement agencies in a particular state agreed on the standards for source training, those standards would have greater worth than ones set by a single agency, in that state. For less populous countries, national training standards should be the goal. The same can be said for source management procedures.

Third, training should only be delivered by a suitably qualified person. How do we know who is qualified to provide source management training? Imagine that the trainer has to provide to a court or an inquest, details of what qualified them to deliver the training. For example, if part of the training consists of a law module, then we would expect to see it delivered by a lawyer, who has specialized in criminal law and preferably, with experience in working with human sources. A divorce lawyer would not be suitable. Trainers must be able to *evidence* why they were suitable to provide that training. Just because they have 'done it' for a few years does not meet the criteria. If using someone from outside the agency, that person should be willing to defend in court the training they provided and their qualifications as a trainer.

Fourth, the content of all training should be retained, and date stamped. An agency should be able to say: 'On this course, on this day, this officer received training on 'X, Y, and Z'. Here are the lesson outcomes and here is the PowerPoint that was used.' We need to be able to evidence what was delivered.

Fifth, training for those officers involved full-time in source management, must include knowledge and the application of that knowledge. Roleplays and scenario-based training forms a critical part of any course. Officers should demonstrate that they can apply the theories they are taught. This will often involve training outside the classroom.

Sixth, developmental training must be made available. Training is not a one-time fix. The agency must be able to provide training to keep an officer's knowledge current, and have the ability to increase their knowledge and skills, as they gain real-world experience on the job.

Seventh, officers of all ranks need appropriate training. There is a limited point in providing training to Handlers if the Authorizing Officer, who is making critical decisions is not trained to make them. Similarly, with the Senior Responsible Officer. We wouldn't let a ship's captain tell the sailor how to steer the ship, if the captain wasn't qualified to do so.

Eighth, where possible we should always seek input from other agencies that are operating in a similar environment. Sharing experiences, shares knowledge. There are many different ways to interact with a source and no one has a monopoly on all the good ideas. In a similar vein, we don't all need to make the same mistake to learn. Sharing our mistakes makes it less likely that others will make them.

A tiered approach

There are advantages to adopting a tiered approach to source management training. First, training is delivered in an appropriate way to meet the officer's needs. Second, resources are not wasted in paying for training that someone does not need. Third, the level to which an officer is trained indicates the difficulty of the task that they can be expected to undertake. There would be additional risks in using a Handler with only basic training to manage a High-Risk source. Four levels of training are suggested as a starting point.

Level One: Human Source Awareness. This course is intended for all members of the agency. It is intended to make staff aware of the definitions and policies about managing human sources. It should enable them to distinguish between a Member of the Public (MoP) and a human source. It should tell them how to submit information from a Member of the Public and who to speak to if they need advice about someone who may be suitable as a human source. It would normally be delivered during recruit training or as an online module. The training would last approximately 3 hours.

Level Two: Human Source Procedures. Level two training comprises a minimum of 24 hours of training and addresses solely the legal and procedural issues for human source management within the agency. It should be aimed at any officer intending to join a Dedicated Source Unit and any officers who will occasionally assist in managing a human source. For example, an officer who has specialist knowledge of money laundering, who will be accompanying a Handler to debrief a source on financial crime. It should include the following topics: relevant intelligence processes and structures, human source definitions, law (including human rights/civil liberties), policy and procedures, source management roles, and records and record keeping. For officers intending to progress to a Dedicated Source Unit completing this course may be immediately followed by the Level Three course.

Level Three: Human Source Management. Level three training is aimed at members of the Dedicated Source Units. After this training, the officers will be deemed competent to manage all sources including those deemed 'High Risk'. This will include sources reporting on organized crime and terrorism. This course will cover the following topics: ethics, anti-corruption, active listening, effective communication, motives and motivation, cognitive debriefing (See Chapter 5) source recruiting, conflict management, and fieldcraft. Identifying and managing risk will be at the core of all aspects of this course. It will also include lessons on using sources in operations and the management of sources reporting on terrorism. There should also be an input from a psychologist on stress management. There should also be input on diversity. Handlers encounter many people from diverse backgrounds and there are many diversity-related issues that they need to be able to recognize.

The level three course will contain some basic elements of psychology, such as relating to communication and motivation. As most will have no prior understanding of these concepts expecting them to advance into more complex theories of psychology at this time, is unrealistic. This course should include both theory and practical exercises.

Not everyone is suitable for the role of managing sources (Henry et al, 2019) (Explored below). This course should be used to identify those officers with any significant shortcomings. Competency-based training is recommended. It is a style of education that focuses on what we can achieve in the workplace, after completing a course. Officers should be assessed against agreed competencies. With competency-based assessment, we either reach the competencies or we don't. It is suggested that a total of ten assessed exercises with seven carried out individually by the officer in a controlled environment, where all their actions can be heard and observed by assessing staff. Three exercises can be carried out in Handler pairs, to assess their behavior working as a team and in a natural environment. Potential Handlers should be assessed against three groups of competencies, and Controllers against an additional fourth group. Group one are the *interpersonal* competencies. These address the Handler's ability to interact appropriately with the human source. Group two are *fieldcraft* competencies These address the Handler's ability to meet safely with the source. Group three are *procedural* competencies. These address the Handler's ability to behave legally and ethically and per agency procedures. Group four are *Controller* competencies. These competencies address supervisory issues. Having completed a Level Three course, the officer will be deemed as being **suitable for appointment** to the role.

For smaller agencies, whose mandate is to investigate local crime problems, this level of training is probably all that their officers will require, provided there are opportunities for continuous professional development. This course takes approximately three weeks to deliver.

Level Four: Proactive Recruitment. The level four course is an advanced course concentrating on the proactive recruitment of sources and contains advanced psychological techniques. It is aimed at Handlers with significant experience who are ready to grasp more advanced concepts and techniques. It is suggested that Handlers have a minimum of two years of full-time handling experience before attending this course. This type of training may not be available to many agencies, as it requires significant levels of subject matter expertise. This course takes approximately two weeks to deliver.

91

Authorizing Officer Training. A separate course should be designed for those performing the roles of Authorizing Officer and/or Designated Responsible Officer. These officers must be trained for their role relating to sources. If they are not, it becomes extremely difficult to defend any decision they have made. How can we decide something if we don't know what we are deciding about? If a senior officer is not willing to undertake this type of training, they are wholly unsuitable for the role. This trait is a clear indicator of how they see the world and conflicts with the attributes that are needed for this role. This training should include an overview of the source management structures, the main problems with sources, ethical decision making, and risk management. Problem-based learning is an effective way to deliver this training.

It is recognized that for many this may seem to be a lot of training. It is. That said, in the USA the military HUMINT collectors' course is 20 weeks. While the role has some differences with that of a Handler, there is significant crossover. Having studied what goes wrong in source relationships, and how unproductive many of these relationships are, it is safe to say that, for the most part, a lot of law enforcement officers have no in-depth understanding of the task they are undertaking. If we are not told anything different, it is easy to fool ourselves that what we are doing, is not only the right way to do something, but the only way to do it. And then we compound this mistake by passing it on to the next generation, and the one after. Training cuts years from the learning process and years of learning the wrong things. We can send officers out equipped to do the job and get the results we want. Or we can send them out without the training they need and wait for it all to wrong.

Handler selection

Not every officer that wants to manage sources is suitable for that role. Without going into all the details of why this is the case, what it comes down to is the fact that some officers do not have the aptitude to do the work safely and effectively. As a general guide, the following figures are useful to bear in mind when selecting officers for the role. About 10 % of officers who want to do the role are naturally good at it. They have high levels of interpersonal skills and can manage the ambiguity that is often present. Instinctively people gravitate towards them and place their trust in them. Training will hone the natural aptitude of these officers.

Another 50% of officers who want to do the role, will have the aptitude to do the role. They need comprehensive training to bring out the best in them and maximize their productivity. These are competent officers and given the time to develop will be good at this role.

The remaining 40 % are *unsuitable* to manage sources. On their best days, with a considerable investment in training, some may scrape over the competence line. However, there will always be additional risks in allowing these officers to manage sources. It is not that they are bad officers. They may be exceptional officers in other roles. However, source management requires specific skills, and these skills cannot be trained, regardless of how much time is invested. Some people can't drive well, so they are likely to be unsuitable for traffic duties. Others can't shoot well so they are not suitable for firearms teams. This needs to be recognized by management when it comes to sources. Training needs to be designed to identify officers that are unsuitable for the role.

Fieldcraft training

If the officers are not trained in fieldcraft they place everyone involved at substantial risk. The extent to which officers need to be trained will be dependent on the operational environment and the level of risk that exists. The Senior Responsible Officer should prepare on an annual basis, a briefing document that provides an assessment of the threats pertaining to sources in their operational area. From that document, the amount of training required can be identified. As a minimum, the time taken to train officers in the basic fieldcraft techniques is 24 hours. Included in this training will be defensive surveillance (how to get to and from a source meeting without being compromised by hostile surveillance), 'cover stories' (a ploy to disguise the true nature of the activity being undertaken), and safe communication methods. It will also include suitable locations to use for meetings, how to use those locations, and under what circumstances to use those meeting places. Regular refresher training in fieldcraft is needed.

Time to develop

With the amount of effort needed to train people, we want to get the maximum amount of work out of them. Following this training, it will probably take another two to three years of gaining on the job experience before we can feel confident that the Handler can manage most sources without the support of a more experienced Handler. The first three years should be used as akin to an apprenticeship with the Handler undertaking increasingly more complex tasks while being continually supported by an experienced Handler. Having completed three years full time, the officer will be deemed as being **experienced** for their role. It is at this stage that the officer is ready for further training. This will be particularly relevant for agencies that our investigating high-level organized crime and terrorism and want to manage High-Risk sources or adopt a proactive recruitment strategy.

For there to be a return in investment and to ensure that standards in the agency our maintained there should be an expectation that the officer will commit a minimum of five years to the role. It is only after *five years* in the role and with continuous professional development that a Handler will be deemed as having **mastered** the role and be suitable as a mentor, the lead Handler with High-risk Sources, capable of being involved in interagency work and able to deploy sources into high-risk operations such as those involving undercover officers. Many of the High-Risk sources that agencies may want to manage have been involved in criminality for a lifetime. They are often highly intelligent, street-smart, and manipulative individuals. It takes a long time to develop the skills necessary to recruit and manage such a person. Driven by ignorance and hubris, sending an officer with limited experience out to manage such a person is negligence.

Each agency needs officers with *expertise.* Officers with the aptitude for working with sources and a desire for professional development, should be provided with opportunities to continue performing duties connected with source management. If this does not happen then knowledge will be continuously lost, and the agency will repeat errors over and over again, as new officers make the same mistakes the more experienced ones already made. Good source Handlers are hard to find, and the agency should do everything in their power to keep officers involved in the role and motivated to do it well. Handlers should be encouraged to seek promotion, bringing their experience to the role of Controller. Unfortunately, many senior managers have no idea of the complexity of the source management task and leave their agency vulnerable by removing those with experience and expertise from their post, as a matter of routine after a very limited time. It is a bit like telling a nurse she does three years learning their role in surgery and then moving them to geriatrics.

Training the source.

Sources need to be trained for their role. The longer the source relationship exists, the greater the amount of fieldcraft that will, of necessity be shared with the source. Although many sources will have an in-depth knowledge of how to keep themselves safe within their criminal environment, their position in that environment changes when they agree to become a source. Handlers must first recognize that the source is likely to have at least some awareness of what they can and cannot do. It is important to consult the source before any task. Moreover, the Handler should document the amount of knowledge that the source has in this regard. An entry in a contact note may read something like: 'Spoke to the source about visiting the Clubhouse. The source stated he had been there many times before and knew the drill for gaining access.' This indicates that the Handler was not asking the source to undertake a task that they were not capable of undertaking. In many cases, the source will have had a lifetime of experiential learning about criminality. However, if this is not the case, then the Handler will have to provide instruction. When providing any instruction, the Handler should avoid the use of any law enforcement jargon, and instead use the language that is common within the circles in which the source operates.

Simple aspects of training that the Handler should provide from the beginning include matters of basic fieldcraft. Some sources may be very cunning, while at the same time making the most fundamental of errors.

If the training involves setting do's and don'ts for the source, each must be accompanied by an explanation. If the source cannot understand why they should do something, they will not do it.

Handlers need to constantly reiterate important messages, especially those that relate to source safety. When a Controller meets with the source, the Controller should check that the source understands the instruction they have been given:

'Did these guys tell you about keeping safe?'

'Yeah.'

'Just run it past me what they told you.'

The Handler provides training and the Controller checks it has been understood. The Controller then completes the appropriate record (a contact note, more later) to confirm the training has been provided and has been understood. A teacher teaches, an examiner examines. The learning is confirmed. Everyone has the proof it has been done.

Conclusion

In this chapter, we have looked at the first two of the three pivotal elements needed to manage a source namely policy and procedures, and training. In the next chapter, we will look at the third – records.

3. Records

*What I argue is that if I'm going to be held accountable
for my actions that I should be allowed to record... my
actions. Especially if somebody else is keeping a record of
my actions.*

Steve Mann (Born 1962)

Introduction

Now the fun starts. We are going to talk about record
keeping. And don't think you can skip this chapter
because this is the area in which most of the mistakes
are made. To put it simply, if you are NOT keeping
records effectively you are NOT managing the source
effectively. There are no 'ifs' or 'buts' about this. For
some, this chapter may read like source management
for kindergarten children. If you read it and think, 'I
knew all that.', that is great! But just check if everyone
involved in the agency knows it all. And you also might
want to be certain that the agency has the structures in
place to make sure these records are being completed
systematically, and to an appropriate standard. This
chapter will outline the reasons why effective records
are essential, what records there should be, and how
and by whom, each record should be completed.

Why keep records?

As we have already discussed one of the key elements
of human source management is 'management' and it

is only by adopting a systematic approach to management, that a source can be managed safely and productively. For there to be effective management we need to record everything that is happening concerning the source. Records facilitate *internal* oversight of the source relationship, by those managers charged with that responsibility. Records facilitate *external* oversight. Whether as a matter of routine or because of an incident of some kind, good records allow someone enquiring about how a source has been managed to see a clear picture from the beginning to the end of the relationship, with that source. The courts are likely to be one place where there is vigorous external oversight.

Records provide proof as to how a source has been managed. All records should be kept to evidential standards. Records ensure that risks are clearly identified and managed appropriately. We will discuss risk management later, but if we do not record what is happening now, it is impossible to identify what might happen in the future. Records protect all the officers in the source management team. If allegations are made about how the source has been managed or about the behavior of any officer involved, then we want to be able to prove what took place. Records prevent corruption. There is a real risk of an officer becoming involved in corrupt behavior when managing a source. Good record-keeping makes most of the types of corruption more difficult and will also provide early warning that something in the relationship is becoming, or has become, corrupt. Records protect the agency as a whole. It is always difficult to ensure that no single officer does something wrong, but if an agency has comprehensive records it can prove that there was not institutionalized or systematic wrongdoing. Good records can also help an agency quantify the benefits that are coming from the use of sources. If we are spending a substantial amount of public money on rewarding sources, then we want to be able to show the public that they obtained value for that expenditure. Records allow managers to readily identify if and when a specific source is being productive. There is little point in engaging the risks of managing a source if there is not sufficient benefit for the agency, at the end of the day. Some Handlers can be very reluctant to stand-down a source. Records can ease this decision, when it is readily apparent that the agency is not getting a return on their investment.

Key principles

There are a few key principles regarding records. First, the agency must keep comprehensive records of all source operations. These records should be kept in a central location. Officers should not be allowed to keep any source records under their control. There is no point in having records where supervisors cannot see them, or where they can be inadvertently or deliberately destroyed. If additional notes or records are kept elsewhere this increases the risks. The agency's in-house email system should not be used as a tool in the management of a source. It is lazy. They present a security risk and are extremely difficult to find if needed at a later date. An agency is likely to have millions of emails. If an email has been used, a copy of it must be kept in the source file. The same goes for handwritten reports and text messages.

Second, all records should be kept securely. Given that there is real potential that if the identity of a source is exposed, they will come to harm, all records should be kept securely, with access strictly limited to a need to know basis. Furthermore, much of the information that sources provide will be extremely sensitive. The agency must protect the source records and the product of source operations. The agency should be able to list who has had access to the identity of a source and when they had access to those details. If an instruction is given by text to a Handler and it relates to a source, a record of it should be entered in the decision log.

Third, all records should be kept to evidential standards. All records should be timed and dated. Each document produced should have a unique number. Given that the primary goal of most information-gathering operations will ultimately be to bring perpetrators to trial, all records should meet evidential standards. This also protects the citizen's rights to a fair trial. Furthermore, all records should be stored where they can be accessed by an agency at a later date, even after the officer has left. One only has to look at how allegedly non-existent records suddenly appeared at The Royal Commission into the Management of Police

Informants in Australia[6] and the impact that had on the credibility of the evidence that had been presented.

Fourth, all records should be in a standardized format. Everyone in the agency should use the same forms. There are no adaptations. We do not have one set of forms for drug units and a different set for gangs. Everyone must complete all forms. Counter-terrorism officers cannot leave out the bits they do not like. When creating these forms all end-users should have input.

Fifth, at the termination of the source all records should be examined to ensure that all the information that has been collected, has been processed into intelligence and is stored legally. The length of time these records are kept for should be stated in the agency's procedures. The standard time should be 7 years. After this time, the source records should be reviewed and unless there are mitigating reasons, they should be destroyed. In most cases, the risks of keeping such records far outweigh any benefits from keeping them. 'Just in case' is not a valid reason to keep a record that might, if exposed, cause someone to lose their life. The longer we keep the records the longer the risk exists of the source's identity being exposed.

Sixth, there should be a regular audit of all source files to ensure that the standards set by the agency are being adhered to, and that officers are not engaging in

---

[6] For further reading on this matter see https://www.rcmpi.vic.gov.au/

unlawful behavior. Furthermore, audit protects civil liberties.

Seventh, good records make statistical data readily available. Data such as the number of sources the agency is managing, the number of meetings that have taken place in an identified period, the amount of money expended, and the ensuing results should all be available to the head of the agency, at the touch of a button. Monitoring what is being done, by whom and what it is achieving, is just one way of reducing the risk of officers being drawn into a situation where citizen's rights are violated.

Eighth, in a paper file, all documents should be stored in reverse chronological order. The most recent document in each category will be at the top. Anyone opening the file can see the current status of the source immediately.

These simple steps help prove that an agency has adopted a proactive approach to addressing civil liberty issues and been proactive in addressing the risk of corruption. In addition, it ensures that the agency is using sources in the most productive way. Furthermore, it is always worth remembering there are defense lawyers out there, willing to exploit any vulnerability to gain an acquittal. Cases should not be lost because of poor law enforcement processes or poor record-keeping. The steps mentioned above significantly mitigate the risk of cases being dismissed purely because of an alleged civil liberty violation or because vital evidence has been lost.

Good records management is knowing what you have, where you have it, how long you have to keep it, and that it is secure where it is.

Computerization

I have just checked my watch and we are definitely in the 21st century. There is no reason why any law enforcement agency in a modern western democracy continues to use a paper-based system to manage sources. The safest and most cost-effective way is to use a purpose-built computerized system. The benefits that can be obtained from a computerized system far outweigh the limited investment required to purchase such a system. There are some things to remember in purchasing such a system. First, do not try and build it yourself. Few agencies have the knowledge of either information technology or source management, to know what needs to go into such a system. There is a lot of specialized knowledge needed in both regards. In a similar vein, the cost of building such a system is likely to be prohibitive. There are various 'off the shelf' products available. Analyze your needs and test what is on offer. Second, make sure the security in the system is strong. Only security cleared agency staff should be able to access the data. Third, there must be a comprehensive audit facility built into the software to record who has created or accessed any document, and the date and time they did so. This must be done to an evidential standard. These are the basics.

There are many more benefits that computerization will bring, and we will discuss some of these as we go through. What makes computerization much more attractive is that it saves the agency considerable amounts of money through time-saving. Using the budget as an excuse not to computerize, is just that, an excuse for negligence. However, not all developing nations can afford the software needed and paper systems remain the only option.

The records

As we have said, not everyone can afford a computerized system, and we know that a lot of others will not bother. What we will illustrate here can be achieved on a paper-based system. The content remains the same.

Personal details. This form contains the personal details of the source. It includes their full name, any previous names, nicknames, or pseudonyms that they use or have used. It also includes their address, their date of birth, their current employment, contact numbers, and the names of immediate family members. Current photos of the source should also be included. This form should be held in a sealed envelope separately from the remainder of the file making it more difficult for anyone to see the true identity of the source. On the front of the envelope should be the unique reference number for the source and any code name they have been allocated.

For example, the source's name may be Samuel Smith but on the front of the envelope, it will say Code Number: H123 and Code Name: Dark Night. The code number and code name (if allocated) are the only details that appear on any other record. Code numbers should not be allocated sequentially, and should not contain any other identifier such as a year of issue or an indicator of the department managing them. Code numbers and names should be centrally allocated, and no code number should be reallocated. Code names should not have any connection to the source. In our example, 'Smitty' would not be a good code name. Furthermore, codenames should be appropriate. They may become public knowledge. So 'Humpty Dumpty' may seem funny at the time, but a judge may not find it quite so funny. For female sources, if using a name, it is better to use a name that sounds gender neutral, such as 'Alex' or 'Jo'. Generally speaking, there are significantly fewer women involved in crime than men, so a female source can be easier to pinpoint. Only the source number will be used on all records of that source. Their real name will not be used anywhere. In larger agencies, this form is held by the Source Administrator.

The Source File

To make it easy, imagine you have a ring binder which will contain the source file. Our first step will be to include several dividers so that we can separate the file into different sections. Section One deals with the registration of the source. Section Two deals with the day-to-day management of the source, Section Three with finance, Section Four with miscellaneous material, and Section 5 with evidential material. We begin with Section One. Each of the forms described below is a separate form. We must always bear in mind that when it comes to disclosure of records, we will want to disclose the minimum necessary to protect the life of the source and to protect methodology.

All these forms are completed using only the code number of the source. Their true identity should not be on these forms. Similarly, the members of the source management team should use their personal operational numbers.

Section One: Registration

Section one deals with the registration of the source for the agency. It includes Applications, Risk Documents, Authorisations, Reviews, Renewals, and Cancellations.

Application. An application to formally register and use the source should be submitted by a Handler, through the Controller to the Authorizing Officer. The application should detail the nature of the investigation on which the source is reporting and how the use of that source will further the investigation. It should give a brief history of the source's circumstances and a synopsis of how the source knows the targets of the investigation. It should address privacy issues and name the primary targets of the investigation. It should give anticipated benefits and relevant timescales. For

108

example, the source will continue to build up a picture of the movements of Garcia, a known dealer, over the next two months.

Where the source is providing information of a more general nature, for example about activities taking place in a 'hard to reach' community, the nature of their reporting and the need for that reporting should be included. This negates allegations that law enforcement activities are targeted at a particular community.

Risk documents. Accompanying the application will be several 'risk documents' identifying the specific risks of managing this source and the control measures in place to manage each risk. One form is used for each risk. A more detailed explanation of risk management is provided below.

Application to recruit. Where an agency has the ability to proactively recruit human sources, agency records should be commenced with details of that individual under recruitment being recorded. The primary purpose of this is the early clarification as to identify whether or not that person is currently, or has ever been previously registered, as a human source, and to deal with whatever matters arise from such an event. This may also help identify if the person is already the subject of another investigation/operation.

If the source intends to enter into a formal *contract* with the agency, the terms of this contract should be attached to the application.

The application, including the risk documents, is submitted by the Handler to the Controller. The Controller will also be handed the envelope containing the true identity of the source. It is the job of the Controller to verify the details contained in the application. They then forward it, and the true identity to the Authorizing Officer.

Authorization. The Authorizing Officer should examine the application with particular reference to the potential benefits of using the source, balanced against the risks that are present. They should consider the extent to which any person's human rights/civil liberties are engaged and that this is proportionate to what the agency is hoping to achieve. The Authorizing Officer should examine the experience and training of both the Handlers and Controller involved. They will be certifying that these officers are suitable to manage this source. Having examined the application, the Authorizing Officer then authorizes the application and sets the date and time of commencement of the authorization and the date and time of termination. A standard period for authorization should be included in the procedures. This would normally be for one year.

The Authorizing Officer will specify the *generic taskings* that the source is to undertake. These answer the question: 'What do I expect the source to achieve during the authorization period.?' They should cover the areas on which the source is expected to report and, in most cases, there will be 5 or 6 generic tasks. They should be sufficiently broad to cover day-to-day reporting, but specific enough to avoid including everything. For example, 'The source will report on the activities of the West End crime gang', would be appropriate, whereas 'the source will report on drug dealing in the City X' is much too vague. These taskings will form part of the source's performance metrics, so preparing them takes some thought. They may include both strategic and tactical objectives.

The Authorizing Officer should also include any additional parameters they deem necessary regarding the nature and limits of the activity that is permitted Where the nature of the activity is more intrusive a higher level of approval should be in place. This would be required for example in deploying a source into a place of worship or where the source is under 18 years of age.

Handlers are notified that they are authorized to manage the source, and the true identity envelope is forwarded to the Source Administrator for retention.

Review. At a time specified by the Authorizing Officer, there should be a mandatory review of the authorization to ensure the source is achieving what was expected. Too often sources are kept 'on the books' simply because no one takes them 'off the books.' This review would normally take place at the midpoint of the authorization. It should include what the source has achieved to date, and how close they are to achieving the identified goals. It should also include any rewards provided to the source and any additional risks. The Authorizing Officer can direct a review at any time or a review can be submitted at any time, if there is a change in circumstances and direction is needed.

Renewal. At the end of the authorization period (normally one year), the Handler must submit either a renewal application or a cancellation. The renewal application will contain the same details as the application together with a break-down of what the source has achieved in the period of authorization. Renewal should not be viewed as a foregone conclusion. The Handler must make the case to renew and the Authorizing officer must again make a judgment based on all the circumstances. If the Authorizing Officer decides to renew, they complete a new authorization. If they decide against, they will direct that a cancellation form is submitted.

Termination. Termination is the formal notification that for whatever reason, the source is no longer being used as a source. In most cases, the source should be informed. This must be completed for every source. It should contain the reasons for termination and what was achieved. If there are any risks in termination these should be detailed on the proper risk document. The termination is approved by the Authorizing Officer. A contact note (later) should reflect that the source has been notified of the termination.

Criminal participation authorization. This is a formal authorization for the source to engage in a criminal act on behalf of the agency. This can only be used if the jurisdiction has legislation that permits this to happen. Too often such conduct is allowed to continue with the Handlers just turning a blind eye to criminality because it is providing benefit to them, in the form of information.

Section Two: Day-to-Day Management.

Section two of the source file is continuously updated. This may be done once a week, once a day, or several times a day, depending on what is happening and how active the source is. It is the responsibility of the Controller to check these records daily. They must identify any issues and either notify the Authorizing Officer or the Handlers depending on the issue. All these forms are completed using only the code number of the source. Their true identity should not be on these forms.

Decision log. The decision log is a record of any decision that has been taken regarding the management of the source. It is sometimes called a policy log. The first entry in the decision log should be a record of the circumstances under which the source was recruited and details of the strategy for short, medium, and long-term objectives regarding the source. All decisions relating to the management of a source should be recorded in a way that *all* those involved in the management, can see them. There is little point in the Authorizing Officer deciding something, if the Handlers cannot see what it is. Decision logs should contain the decision that has been made and the reasons for that decision. Decision logs are an essential part of risk management and they hold officers accountable for their actions. An example of what should be included is, in a case where a serious threat to the source exists, the Authorizing Officer may decide that the source is not to be met for a given period. The nature of the threat and the rationale for the decision will both be included.

A record of any meeting or discussion about the source will go into the decision log. Sometimes people get confused about what to record, where. To make it easy to remember, in source management, any discussion about the source, when they are not present, goes in the decision log. If the source *is present*, then it goes in a contact note.

Contact notes. A contact note contains details of everything that occurs during a contact with a source. Each contact note should have a unique number. This may be sequential for that source or randomly generated by the computer. They will include all the details of who was present and everything about the source's management and welfare. Each report will include, the date and time of the contact and when the Controller approved that contact, who contacted who, the means used, in person or phone, the duration of the contact, and its specific location. It will also include the date and time the contact note was completed and submitted. In face to face meetings the details of all vehicles used in the meeting will be recorded, the identity of the officers that were involved will be recorded. This should include details of officers that were present for security. If the source is having any sort of problem, whether directly related to their role as a source or not, it should be recorded here. Any taskings that are given to the source should be included and their response to being given the task. If they have concerns about it, these should be noted.

Any training given to the source should be recorded, each time it is delivered. Where payment is provided, or any gift given to the source this should be included. Details of any expenditure should also be included. If a video or audio recording has been made of the contact, the contact note should include this fact. If the source is corresponding using email, (a covert account having been set up and used exclusively by that source.) then copies of all emails sent to, or from, the source should be attached to a contact note.

Contact notes do not have to be written in any particular style. They are intended to provide an account of what happened, not a literary masterpiece. The information can be recorded in bullet points and having a consistent structure will make it easier to read and lessen the chances of material being omitted. Each contact requires a separate contact note, though one note may suffice for a series of telephone calls over a limited period. Handlers should vary who completes the contact note. This helps ensure integrity and shares the workload. Contact notes should be completed as soon as practical after the contact has taken place, and within 72 hours as a maximum. When completed, the contact note should be submitted to the Controller for verification.

On receipt of the contact note, the Controller should study the contact note to ensure it is comprehensive, and to identify any potential problems with the source or any risks that may be present. Where there are audio or video recordings the Controller, should, on a random basis check the content of the contact note and the content of the recording are comparable. Where a Controller attends a source meeting, they should complete the contact note. It is the responsibility of the Controller to highlight to the Authorizing Officer any issues of concern, contained in the contact note. There is no expectation that an Authorizing Officer reads every contact note, for every source.

Contact notes are an essential tool to manage a source. They ensure that a consistent approach is adopted. They are useful in identifying, quantifying, and managing risk. Someone should be able to read the contact notes and have a clear picture of the career of that source from beginning to end.

Terms and conditions. If it is agency procedure that the source signs terms and conditions these are included here and cross-referenced in the contact note for the day they were signed.

Information submission. An example of a standard information submission is given below. Section 1 provides administrative details. Each information submission is given a unique reference number. This adds layers to security and helps when it comes to protecting from unnecessary disclosure. It is completed by the first Handler named in Section 1 and checked by the second Handler. Section 1 is completed once for one contact. Section 2 deals with the information provided by the source. As the source may provide any number of pieces of information during a meeting Section 2 may be repeated with a new Section 2 for each new piece of information. Again, this allows for greater protection concerning disclosure. Where the $\pm$ sign appears on the form, this indicates this section may be repeated any number of times. Ideally, on a computerized system, the computer generates an additional box.

The information submission should allow for both 'source comment' i.e. what their take is, on the information, and any comment from the Handler who is submitting it. If there is a particular risk surrounding this piece of information, it should be stated. For example, a piece of information may be time-sensitive and require immediate action. Alternatively, with another piece of information immediate action may expose the source. Comments to address these issues inform the Intelligence Unit on how to better manage the product.

When a new entity is discussed with the source, it is the responsibility of the Handler to obtain the maximum amount of detail about that entity. For example, if a source has provided the name of a new drug dealer, the Handler should attempt to fully identify the person with details such as age, addresses, vehicles used, and a description being entered into the relevant data fields.

The Handler may suggest a grading for the information. However, it is the responsibility of the Intelligence Unit to grade (See Chapter 6) the subsequent intelligence reports. They have insight into the bigger picture. Where there is a significant disparity between the gradings provided by the Handler in the information submission and those allocated by the Intelligence Unit in the related intelligence report the Controller should seek out the reasons. For example, if the Handler has graded a piece of information B2 and on the related intelligence report it is graded B5, the Handlers need to know why it has been lowered, because it may bring into question what is happening with the source. The source may be deliberately misleading the Handlers. The comparison of the gradings also serves to ensure that the Handlers are less likely to lose perspective concerning the source: 'My source always tells the truth. My source is always right.'

When all pieces of information have been written up, the Handler forwards the information submission to the Controller who checks it for content. It is the Controller's job to ensure data quality. If the Handlers have left stuff out, the Controller should be raising it.

Human Source Information Submission	
SECTION 1 COMPLETION DETAILS	
Information Submission Reference(ISR) Number:	
Date information received:	Time information received:
Date Submitted:	Time Submitted:
Handler (1) Number:	Handler (2) Number:
Source Code Number:	Source Code Name:

SECTION 2 INFORMATION	±
Information:	
Provenance:	
Source Comment:	
Handler Comment:	
Are there any risks associated with this piece of information?	

ENTITIES	
Person	±
Location	±
Thing	±
Event	±
Vehicle	±
Telecoms	±

Credibility:	Validity:	Dissemination:
Controller Comment:		

Figure 3.1   Information Submission

Intelligence report. The agency should have a standard intelligence report that is used for all intelligence reporting. The intelligence report should have a unique reference number (URN). Nowhere on the intelligence report should there be an indication of the origin of the intelligence. Only the Intelligence Unit should be able to link the URN to the origin of the report. The source management team will be able to see all intelligence reports submitted by their source.

Intelligence Report		
SECTION 1 COMPLETION DETAILS		
Unique Reference Number:		
Date information received:	**Time information received:**	
Date Submitted:	**Time Submitted:**	
Submitting Officer		
SECTION 2 INTELLIGENCE		
Intelligence		
Intelligence Unit Comment		
ENTITIES		
Person		±
Location		±
Thing		±
Event		±
Vehicle		±
Telecoms		±
Credibility:	Validity:	Dissemination:
SECTION 3 ACTION		
Intelligence Reposited **For Reference Only**	Intelligence Reposited **For Development**	Intelligence Reposited **For Action**

Figure 3.2   Intelligence Report

In the Intelligence Unit, it is the job of an Intelligence Officer to analyze the information submission and select a form of words that is suitable for inclusion on an intelligence report. They should sanitize the intelligence in a way that makes it all but impossible to identify where that intelligence originated. One

120

information submission may produce numerous intelligence reports. They then grade that intelligence report and decide who the intelligence report is to be disseminated to and provide instruction as to what should be done with it. All intelligence reports are reposited into the agency's Intelligence Repository where it can be accessed at any time later. If there is nothing further to be done with it, it will be marked for reference only. If it requires further investigation it is disseminated to the relevant unit or the most relevant agency. If it is deemed as *actionable* it is disseminated to an officer of sufficient rank to ensure that the report is actioned.

As the name infers, *actionable intelligence* is about taking action concerning the intelligence obtained. Actionable intelligence is defined as 'Intelligence with sufficient specificity and detail to implement immediate action by a law enforcement agency.' For intelligence to be deemed actionable it means there is little or no need for further research or investigation. For example, 'There is a stolen car in the warehouse at 64 Main Street' or 'There are ten kilos of cocaine at Apartment, 163, High House, Anytown.' Actionable intelligence can be acted upon either by taking overt executive action or sometimes through a covert response. Where intelligence is disseminated to be actioned, implicit in its dissemination is that the action will be carried out forthwith. A lot of intelligence is time-sensitive.

Handlers may submit draft intelligence reports. This can aid considerably in the sanitization process, but Handler's may also be reckless or over-protective of what is disseminated. The Intelligence Unit is there to make an objective assessment. Figure 3.3 shows the process of information collection through to action. The named person on the left does the tasks on the right.

Figure 3.3 Information Submission Process

Section Three: Finance

All financial transactions relating to the management of the source should be recorded in this section of the file. The management of money is one of the most common ways that corruption occurs. These records must be meticulous.

Source expenditure This will include a summary of all payments made directly to the source and include both cash payments and other monetary instruments. It will include expenditure on gifts for the source.

Date	Remuneration	Expenses	Vouchers	Gifts	Comment
May 5	$50	$10			Travel to meeting
May 12			$20		Phone
May 21	$50				Meeting
May 30	$40				Meeting
April 6			£20		Phone

Table 3.1   Source Expenditure

Handling expenses A register of expenses incurred in the management of the source should also be maintained. Source meetings often take place in hotel rooms or coffee shops, and we need to know how much we are spending on these types of things. The Controller may also wish to keep a record of how many man-hours are expended on each source. While this will at best be a rough estimate, it does help inform decisions around if the source represents value for money. Where a credit card has been used the record should stipulate which card was used, and it should be cross-referenced in the Controller's accounts.

Receipts. If the agency policy is that financial payments are signed for by the source, the signed receipt should be stored here.

Monetary reward application. Where the information from a source has led to a notable success the Handler may wish to apply for a financial reward in recognition of the source's work. The application should be stored here, together with the decision. The date and time the reward was paid should be attached.

Non-Monetary rewards. Where the information from a source has led to a notable success the Handler may wish to apply for a reward in recognition of the source's work. However, in some cases, a monetary reward may be inappropriate, or a non-monetary reward may be either more suitable, or more desired by the source. A lot of the time a source will seek to have charges withdrawn or a letter submitted to the court to obtain a lower sentence. All documentation of this type of reward, should be kept here. Furthermore, if such a reward has been seen outside the agency, details of who has seen it should be included in the record.

Section Four: Miscellaneous

Section Four holds much of the documentation that is ancillary to manging the source proficiently. These are some of the records that will be included there.

Taskings. Where specific taskings are provided by the Intelligence Unit or other units, a copy of those taskings should be included here. This also refers to taskings sent by other agencies. The results of the tasking should be paired with the original document.

Enhanced profile. The purpose of an enhanced profile is to aid in the proactive tasking of human sources across the agency. Due to the volume of data potentially involved, it only works properly when using a computerized system. Enhanced profiling stems from two factors. First, as Handlers, we do not know what information the source may have access to, and second, as Handler's we do not know what someone else in the agency may be looking for, now or in the future. With creating an enhanced profile, we bring these two things together. The enhanced profile is a comprehensive list of all the source's associates and places they have frequented throughout their life. It will include places they lived, schools they attended, places they have worked, and prisons in which they have served time. It will include details of their lifestyle, their hobbies, and any skills they may have. The enhanced profile is created to maximize the potential for tasking and to facilitate agency-wide deployments. For example, if the agency is investigating a murder in a particular area of a city, the system can be searched for every source that is connected with that area. These sources can then be deployed to assist in gathering information about the crime. Enhanced profiles take time to build up, but once they are created, they can have considerable utility concerning proactive tasking. They move the agency into being much more proactive than reactive and are worth the initial effort.

Enhanced profiles for the whole agency should be held by the Source Administrator. This means that any Investigator who may require a source has a specific point of contact to see if the agency has a source. The

Investigator provides the Source Administrator with their requirement and the Administrator identifies potential sources. They then inform the Controller of the request. The Controller decides whether or not the source will be used.

Performance indicators. Performance indicators evaluate the success of an organization or a particular activity. Measuring performance for both sources and the officers managing them can be difficult. Care must be taken to avoid performance being measured solely in terms of the quantity of intelligence received. Consideration should always be given to the quality of that intelligence and the relevance of that intelligence for the agency. However, a good starting place to measure performance is through the number and type of intelligence reports that have been produced from the source over a given period. Intelligence reports are completed independently of the source management team, by the Intelligence Unit and therefore, the results are likely to be more objective. Four main types of intelligence can be counted. First intelligence reports that address the *generic tasks* that were decided upon authorization. The agency said it wanted intelligence on these matters and the source has produced 'X' amount of intelligence reports, on these matters. They are producing what we asked for. Second, intelligence reports that are *incidental* to normal source reporting. As a result of the lives they live, sources often hear and see a lot of things that are of interest, but lie outside of their expected reporting area. While we will take this information from the source, it should not be viewed as part of normal performance indicators. We will take

126

it, but we did not request it. However, if the information that the source provides leads to action, then that should be recognized. We may not have asked for it, but it had tangible utility for us. The third type of intelligence reports that are useful as performance indicators are those as a result of *specific tasks* which are outside normal areas of reporting. For example, there may be a serious incident for which Investigators need intelligence. We asked the source to find out about it. If they provide intelligence that is an indicator of good performance. If they do not, it is considered part of their normal functioning to try and find out. Fourth are operational tasks. These are about getting the source to do things for us. They occur when a source provides necessary support to an operation. This may involve, for example, deploying a source into a bar on a particular evening to see if a suspect is present, to facilitate their arrest. The level of effort the source makes in support of this task is critical in deciding whether or not it meets a performance criterion. The key element here, and with incidental reporting, is the idea of above and beyond. There are things we expect the source to do. If they make an additional effort their performance should be recognized accordingly. Some of these call for professional judgment. If officers are professionally trained those judgments will be objective. If the person making the judgment does not have the training needed, they will be laden with their cognitive biases and personal values. Table 3.2 summarises the four areas of performance.

Performance Indicators			
Category	Descriptor	Type	Scored
Generic	Reporting against tasks identified in the source authorization.	Strategic intelligence	Yes
		Tactical intelligence	Yes
Incidental	This is information they bring in that they just happen to find out. For example: 'I heard their was a stolen car hidden in that garage.'	Intelligence for record purposes	No
		Intelligence actioned	Yes
Specific	Tasked to obtain information against a specific crime or incident. For example, Do they know anything about the murder outside The Sportsman Bar?	Deployed	No
		Intelligence submitted	Yes
Operational	Actions or reporting carried out in support of an operation For example, triggering a surveillance operation.	Critical	Yes
		Routine	No

Table 3.2   Performance Indicators

Handlers should always ensure that *all* information the source provides is recorded. If they do not, much of what the source does is not recognized. If a Handler is asking a source a question relating to an investigation and the source answers it, an intelligence report should be completed. For example, 'Do you know where Pedro Garcia lives?' 'Yes. He lives at 46, Church Street, Mossville.' The Handler then submits an information submission stating this and an intelligence report is completed.

Periodic achievement summary. This is a list of what the source has achieved. One should be able to read this record and see how the source is performing. It should be kept up to date and include the number of intelligence reports and the results of any of those reports that have been actioned. This will include details of any persons arrested and/or charged with offenses, properties searched, and contraband

128

recovered. Where intelligence was disseminated for action and that action was not carried out, it should be noted here. Cognizance should always be taken of the number of intelligence reports from the source on which action was taken but that failed to produce the expected results. This may be an indicator of the source not producing accurate information. In some cases, it may be an indication that the agency could not successfully complete the action. A search may have missed material. This summary should be attached to any review of the source.

Request to see the true identity of the source. Any request to see the true identity of a source should be made in writing through the Source Administrator, together with the justification for making the request. A source's true identity should only be divulged on a strictly need to know basis. A copy of the request and the subsequent decision is retained. By examining the source file, the name of everyone who knows the source's identity should be apparent.

Analytical products. All analytical products connected with the recruitment or management of the source are stored in this section. If the source has recruited as a result of a proactive recruitment operation the 'targeting file' will be held here.

Audit. The record of any audit of the source that has been carried out is included here. An explanation of the auditing process is included below

Source calendar. This is a simple tool that helps in the day-to-day management of a source. Handlers cannot be expected to remember important dates in the life of a source. Having a year planner helps the Handler remember significant dates. For example, the source may be going for two weeks' holiday in July, so the Handler needs to remember the source will not be available for tasking. Similarly, the source may have an important family event and it is good source management to remember about that event. If it is important for the source, it is important for the Handler.

Section 5 Evidential record

As we have already discussed all records need to be kept to evidential standards. Section 5 contains records specific to evidence provided by the source.

Submitted items register. There should be a record, in chronological order, of every item that the source has either, directly handed to the Handlers, or caused to come into the Handler's possession. For example, at a meeting, the source may hand over a flash drive containing a download he has made from a computer, or they may leave some items at a prearranged collection point for Handlers to pick up later. It is the decision of the Controller as to what happens to the actual items and their decision is entered here.

If the source provides an item that is likely to be tendered in evidence the item should be stored as per normal agency procedures for evidence handling, with a record of it being entered on the submitted items register. Consultation should take place with prosecutors as to if, and how, that item can be tendered in evidence, without exposing the identity of the source. It will not be easy.

Any gift given to the Handlers should be entered in this register together with how that gift has been disposed of.

Original notes. As we will discuss later because of the nature of memory we have no choice but to use some kind of tool to help us remember everything that the source is telling us. Ideally, audio recordings are the most practical way of doing this. (We will explore why in depth below.) Video recorders are also good but exceedingly difficult to use from a practical perspective. An audio recorder can be carried easily in a pocket. If an audio recording is made it should be kept. If software is being used for source management, the sound recording should be uploaded as an attachment to the contact note. If it is not a hard copy of the tape must be stored. The same tape should never be used for different sources and the recording device should always be encrypted and wiped after each use. Controllers should as a matter of routine, check the content of information submissions and contact notes against the audio recording.

Where handwritten notes are made, the original notes must be stored. These have evidential value. The notes should be removed from the notebook in which they were made. There is always a risk of a notebook being lost and the less that is in it, the better. Under no circumstances should one notebook be used for several different sources. This is poor fieldcraft and endangers the life of sources. Encrypted, electronic notebooks are a much better solution.

A list of all original notes should be kept in the file so that material can be easily found. If software is being used, a copy of the note should be scanned and attached to the contact note.

Officers should not make any record about any aspect of the management of a source in their official notebook, journal, diary, or daybook. These are all standard documents that officers use daily to record what they have done during a particular duty shift. Source records should be kept together. These documents remain, for the most part, under the control of individual officers. An officer may if they must, make a note in their notebook that they met with a particular source at a particular time. If this must be done, then the only thing that should be written is the code number of the source. All other details go in the contact log. If they attend a meeting about the source this goes in the decision log. This problem is much less likely to have relevance if the agency is using Dedicated Source Units. However, even a mere reference to a source during court proceedings may lead to unwanted, potential challenges from a lawyer for the identity of the source to be disclosed. Again, encrypted electronic notebooks provide greater security.

Recording debriefs

In Chapter 5 we will examine the process of debriefing a source. There is one related topic that is best discussed here, as it is a decision that has to be made by the Senior Responsible Officer: How will the agency record contacts with sources? No matter how good a Handler thinks their memory is, no Handler can retain accurately what they have been told during a source debrief.[7] The longer the debrief is the less that will be retained. Accepting then that the Handler needs a method to aid their memory. The choices begin essentially with a simple binary option: do Handler's use hand-written notes or some type of audio/visual device? While this may seem a relatively easy decision there are a lot of complexities to it.

We will begin with *handwritten notes*. First, they seem easy to use and there is no question of legality. The only legal issue is that they are original material and must be kept as best evidence. Now we need to look at the problems. First, they can easily be lost and anyone finding them can read them. Second, note-taking cannot possibly keep up with the speed of speech. Third, note-taking is a distraction, one Handler needs to be totally focussed on what the source is saying, while the other Handler needs to focus on providing security and providing back up in attending to the needs of the source. Fourth, given the fact that many

---

[7] Lamb, Orbach, et al. (2000) found that even with note taking at least 25% of the available detail obtained was not included in later reporting.

debriefs take place in settings such as in darkened car parks or whilst driving, it can be difficult for a Handler to make comprehensive notes. Furthermore, if the debrief is held in a public place it will look unusual to others present if someone appears to be writing down everything another person is saying. Using hand-written notes is an easy option but substantial amounts of information will be lost even if comprehensive notes are made throughout the debriefing.

Typing notes directly into a computer/mobile phone is another option but again this is limited by the speed at which the Handler can type. Handwriting notes into an *electronic notebook/diary* has distinct advantages, foremost of these is security. If the notebook is lost it cannot be read, and the data can be erased remotely. There are a limited number of such encrypted notebooks available. Second, good electronic notebooks automatically date stamp entries keeping all entries to evidential standards. Third, electronic data is easy to store and easy to search. Records can be kept almost indefinitely. Fourth, with advances in technology, some software programs are now capable of turning handwritten documents into type. This can save time later, and a lot of money over a year. Fifth, if the notebook is on-line, it means that data can be instantaneously sent to a remote location with no need to interrupt the debrief. Similarly, if a decision needs to be taken, the Controller can send back permission, and all this is recorded in one secure place. Finally, if the Handler is using an electronic notebook the source can write or draw in it if needed. Everything is kept together in one place. Electronic notebooks are useful even when the agency decides to audio record meetings.

Audio recording of source debriefs should be considered best practice provided the agency has invested in the right equipment to do it effectively and securely. A $20 audio-recorder bought on eBay will fail to pick up what needs to pick up and will likely break down at some critical point. Using a mobile phone needs care, as many phones automatically save and upload data to the cloud. Using recording devices allows the Handler to focus their attention entirely on the source. This ensures better rapport and the ability to focus on exactly what the source is saying. Audio recordings also allow the Controller to listen later to the meeting, if this is required.

There are some issues with audio recordings. First, it may not be legal, a situation that only arises if it is done outside the knowledge of the source. Second, if the source is aware of the recording, there can be a temptation for the source or the Handler to play to the recorder. Most of the time it is better if an agreement to record meetings is made early on in the relationship, and the issue not raised again. When it comes to writing up what has been recorded the Handler will have to spend the same amount of time as the debrief or more, going through the recording and extrapolating the content. For most Handler's the first few times they do this, they are surprised at how much they have missed or forgotten. Once made audio recordings should be retained to evidential standards.

Audio recordings capture source debriefs in there native state. There is no censoring, nor abridgment, to take out the type of language used. For the most part, Handlers are conversing with sources who do not use 'professional' language. While many things would be unacceptable for an officer to say in public, the nature of conversations with a source means that the language used may be more 'interesting' than would normally be used. The conversation with a source should sound much more like a conversation between friends, than a workplace conversation. Swearing may occur from time to time, and comments may be made that if used elsewhere would be deemed inappropriate. It must be remembered that the Handler is performing a role that has significant differences from that of a normal law enforcement officer. If a Handler has to be concerned about recordings being used against them for some trivial statement made, then the conversation will be stifled and the flow of information will be reduced.

If an agency decides to audio-record source debriefs then this should be done for *all* sources, at all times. It is not a matter of deciding to record on an occasional basis. Sporadic recording begs the questions: 'Why did you decide to record this source, on this day?' and 'Why did you not record that source, on that day?' It leaves the agency open to allegations of covering up or hiding material. In addition, the agency must decide if all telephone contacts will be recorded. While this is undoubtedly best practice, logistically it can be difficult. Where it can be done it should be done, and when it isn't done the contact note should reflect why it wasn't done.

Video recording is the most accurate method of recording a source debriefing but is rarely possible because of operational constraints. Where there are an opportunity and potential benefit, a source debriefing may be arranged where a video-recording can be made. Video recordings allow others to examine the body language of both the source and the Handlers during the debrief. This can be useful for example, if there are concerns about the source's mental health and a psychologist wants to see how they come across. It can also be useful in identifying where the source may not be being truthful.

Regional records

Where a large number of agencies are working in a similar geographical area, a centralized clearinghouse for all the agencies is highly recommended. An agreement is made that one agency holds the true identities of all registered sources in that area. It will normally be the agency with the most resources as there will be costs involved. This prevents two agencies from running the same source, at the same time, and it allows agencies to weed out sources who are dangerous. During the application process, the details of the source are sent to the central clearing, to be checked to see if they are or have been previously registered as a source, and if there have been any problems with that source. Processes are put in place to deal with any conflict, but the details of the source are not shared with any of the other agencies.

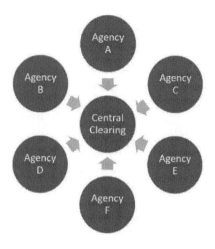

Figure 3.3 Centralised Clearing

Managing Risk

When it comes to managing sources, it is critical to get the balance right between the benefits that can be gained from the source, and the risks involved in managing the source. Within law enforcement, risk management is a poorly understood concept. Sometimes all that is done concerning risk is tokenism. While there is insufficient space here to provide a comprehensive explanation[8] of how to manage the risks with sources, there are a few general pointers. Risks should be managed in a way that ensures compliance with local legislation. This will include privacy legislation, health and safety legislation, and

---

[8] The book 'Invest Now or Pay Later: The management of risk in covert law enforcement' does provide such. (Buckley 2008)

138

any local laws that pertain to managing sources. The method used for managing risk should be an internationally recognized method, such as contained in the International Standards Organization ISO 31018. There should be agreed vocabulary to describe risks within the agency. Risk should always be stated using two terms *likelihood* (probability) the chances of the thing happening, and *consequences* (impact) the result of it happening. Values for likelihood and consequences should be agreed with five levels for each. With likelihood, these will be very low, low, medium, high, and very high. These values indicate the chances of the risk materializing over the time the source is being managed.

Likelihood Values	
Value	Meaning
Very Low	Under the existing circumstances there is no evidence to indicate the likelihood of such an event under the existing circumstances it is assessed that the event is unlikely to occur within the relevant time period.
Low	On the evidence available and under the existing circumstances it is assessed that such an event is less likely to occur than occur at a site similar to this, within the relevant time period.
Medium	On the evidence available and under the existing circumstances, it is assessed that the circumstances exist where the event may occur at a similar site to this, within the relevant period.
High	On the evidence available and under the existing circumstances it is assessed that the event is more likely to occur than not at a site similar to this and within the relevant period.
Very High	On the evidence available and under the existing circumstances it is assessed that the event will almost certainly occur at a site similar to this within the relevant period.

Table 3.3 Likelihood Values

There will be a broad range of potential consequences that must be specified. These can be covered across four areas. *Reputation* – the reputational damage to the agency. For example, if it becomes public knowledge that Handlers have been involved in a corrupt relationship. *Operational* – the operational harm to the agency such as the compromise of investigations. For example, if the source has lied and this compromises charges that have been laid. *Physical Harm* – the injury happening to any person including the source. For example, if the identity of the source is compromised and they are attacked. *Economic* – the potential financial cost to the agency if the risk materializes. For example, if there is a lawsuit against the agency because the source has been compromised.

Impact Values				
Values	Economic	Reputation	To the Person	Operational
Very low	Less than $1000	Embarrassment at local level	Distress to the individual	Minimal Exposure of Methodology
Low	Less than $10000	Significant Embarrassment at local level	Minor Injury	Prejudicial to the investigation of crime
Medium	Less than $100,000	Embarrassment at National Level	Injury requiring treatment	Cause damage to operational effectiveness
High	Less than $1,000,000	Significant Damage To Service	Significant lasting injury	Cause significant damage to operational effectiveness
Very High	Greater than $1,000,000	Irreparable Damage to Service	Death	Causes exceptionally grave damage to op. effective.

Table 3.4 Impact Values

A simple model that will guide an officer identifying all the potential risks is known as **3 P LEM**.

It has six areas of risk. **P**ublic risks – How would the public view what the law enforcement agency is doing? Think in terms of corruption, wasting resources, etc. **P**hysical risks – Will anyone get hurt? Think about the source being attacked or the Handlers attacked on a meeting with the source. **P**sychological risks – Will anyone be psychologically damaged as a result of the relationship. Perhaps the source has been pressurized into the role, or they have existing mental health problems. **L**egal risks – Is there a conflict with the law or agency policy, in what is proposed? Are their Human Rights related risks? Is the source continuing to break the law? **E**conomic risks – What are the potential financial implications? Perhaps the source is a wealthy businessperson and if compromised he may sue the agency for the loss of his business. **M**oral and Ethical – What moral or ethical dilemmas are involved? Perhaps the source is reporting on their spouse. We may be responsible for the break-up of a marriage. While occasionally risks cross from one area into another, if this model is used, then it is unlikely that risks will be missed.

Where a risk is documented it can be *managed* in one of four ways, First, it can be *avoided*. The proposed course of action is not followed. It is just too dangerous to continue with what has been proposed. Second, it can be *retained*. We accept there is a risk but the cost of doing anything outweighs the potential loss. We are prepared to take the hit. Third, the risk can be *transferred*. The financial cost of the event going wrong is transferred to another party. We do this with car insurance. If we have an accident our insurer picks up the cost. Of course, we still have to drive carefully. This usually happens when two agencies co-handle a source and one agency agrees to cover any financial risk. It does not happen often. Fourth, the risk can be *treated*. This involves putting in place a series of control

141

measures to reduce the likelihood (containment) and/or the consequences (contingency). Treating the risk will be the most common strategy. Each risk should be clearly documented in the source file.

Risk Type		Risk Number	
RISK ASSESSMENT			
Risk Identified	There is a risk that....which may lead to....		
Probability	Values very low to very high		
Areas of Impact: *Reputation Operational Physical Economic*	Each area stated in values of very low to very high.		
Overall Impact	A summary of the four areas given as very low to very high.		
Evidence	A short paragraph justifying how the probability and impact values have been arrived at.		
Additional Information			
RISK OWNERS			
	Persons stated by name or role.		
RISK MANAGEMENT			
Management Method	This risk will be: (Avoided, Retained, Transferred, or Treated)		
Control Measures *Containment Contingency*	(If any) Written in bullet points under the following headings:		
Date	Date documented prepared.		

Figure 3.4 Risk Document

Figure 3.4 shows a form that can be used to document the risk. We complete one form for each risk. If you

142

have more than 20 risks identified, it is a clear indicator the source is probably too risky to manage.

Risk should be continuously monitored and updated at each review. This form is simple to complete and helps avoid human error. This of course assumes that the officers have been trained in risk management. Effective training will take approximately 16 hours. All members of the source management team need to be trained. It is negligent not to provide the training and, in some jurisdictions, may amount to a criminal offense.

Audit

For many agencies, the task of managing sources is a task that is routinely carried by officers with few checks as to how well the overall management system is functioning. A mindset will often prevail that: 'As long as things appear to be operating without a problem, then there is no need to upset the applecart by checking to see if there is.' All too often anyone that suggests such action is perceived as working to some personal agenda, or inference is drawn that the officers involved must be suspected of doing something wrong. This is a flawed way of thinking. We need to check how things are being done, so that we can identify where they might go wrong, before they go wrong. Carrying out an audit of how sources are being managed involves looking at the source management system in its entirety, and also regularly examining how individual sources are being managed on a case-specific basis.

143

Often, within an agency's source processes there are good and bad practices and while finding the good is always reassuring, finding the bad, at an early stage, is much better than letting it continue. Every day newspapers carry stories of source management cases that have gone wrong, in a way that could and should have been identified, much earlier than it was. It is better to do an audit now, rather than such an audit being carried out in the public domain when something criminal or tragic has occurred.

Audits should be carried out by a person independent of the operation. If we are auditing the whole source management system, we will probably need an external expert. We rarely have sufficient expertise within our agency to carry out such a wide review. It is also a lot more likely that an external auditor will provide an accurate report, free from internal pressure or bias.

Audits can be carried out on a random basis. A source file is selected and reviewed. This may involve a review of only the records, or it may include interviews with the source management team. In more extreme cases it may involve meeting with the source, though this would be the exception rather than the norm. An audit may be carried out covertly where there is suspicion of wrongdoing. The head of the agency should always be able to access any source record, without the need to inform the Source Management Team. Again, this should be the exception rather than the rule. We do not want to alienate officers.

Many things are likely to be uncovered in an audit. First, is wrongdoing. The extent of such wrongdoing will vary from minor failings in record keeping to potentially criminal actions. It is better for everyone involved that corrective measures are quickly put in place for the minor issues. Any major ones should be referred for investigation, while at the same time measures need to be put in place to manage any associated risks to the source.

Second, misinterpretation and misunderstandings of the agency's source procedures. Many police procedures are poorly written and open to misinterpretation, this leaves the agency, its members, and the public vulnerable. Finding shortcomings in the application of procedures, at an early stage, means that corrections can be made before harm results.

Third, we will find that members of the public (MoPs) are being managed as if they were sources, but that the officers involved have never properly documented these people as sources. Shortcuts are made to the system and officers are lazy about doing the paperwork. 'He is not a source. I only speak to him on the phone.' 'He is just a guy that calls me up. I know him from the bar I go to.' We have already discussed why this happens and the need to distinguish between members of the public giving information, and human sources. This type of wrongdoing is most likely to appear when auditing the intelligence management system. Fourth, an audit will identify officers who are being productive and managing sources effectively, and it will identify officers who are merely 'talking the talk' or that have a cavalier attitude to the rules.

Fifth, an audit may identify sources who are playing the system. Many sources are very productive, but many others are manipulating the agency. Handlers can lose their objectivity and none of us want to believe we can be fooled, especially by someone we may hold in contempt. An audit may also identify where the risks of managing a particular source have not been rigorously evaluated. The agency may be managing a source that they really should have nothing to do with, because they are likely to cause real harm. Many will be familiar with the case of James 'Whitey' Bulger and the damage he did to the reputation of the agency who managed him. Damage like this is unlikely to be forgotten or disappear.

Sixth, an audit may reveal that potential information is missed by the Handlers or that a significant amount of information submitted by the Handlers never gets to where it needs to go. Furthermore, an audit may uncover that while information may have gotten to the people who needed it, they do nothing with it. It was never exploited. A source risked their life to provide it and the agency used resources to collect and process it, but it was just wasted. This can be damaging when something bad has happened and people were hurt, and it is discovered that the agency had prior warning that was not acted upon. There is truly little that will make an agency look quite as bad as the discovery that the agency could have prevented the incident but didn't. We can all remember the allegations that there was prior intelligence about the 9/11 attacks.

Seventh, audit may identify sources who could be used much more effectively who could be tasked in a more productive way against identified priorities. Few agencies manage their sources in a proactive way that adheres to the principles of intelligence-led policing.

Eight, where an agency is managing a large number of sources and different officers are responsible for awarding payments, audit may identify inconsistencies in why and how much sources receive as financial rewards. If there is not an efficient way of tracking source money across the agency, then be prepared for the worst.

Agencies are often reluctant to undertake audits out of fear for what they may find or because of the hostility with which such an undertaking may be met. However, it is better to know that problems exist. And it is also nice to know that things are working properly. Audits also act as a significant deterrent as regards wrong. If we think there is a good chance we will be caught, hopefully, we are less likely to misbehave. Regular audits will also raise standards. Common problems can be identified, and training modified to eradicate the problem.

Where a significant problem has been identified and an investigation is being carried out by Internal Investigations, it is highly recommended that at least one of the officers involved in the investigation is trained in source management. This ensures objectivity and allows for a better understanding of the nuances involved in working with sources. Furthermore, untrained officers should not be interviewing a source as this may lead to the compromise of that source. There is a mistaken belief that the investigation of an officer, trumps the safety of a source. This is rarely, if ever, the case. The rule of thumb here is: If this were a member of the public under investigation, would we expose the source? And if we do expose the source, are we in a position to protect them?

Conclusion

Now that we can see the amount of paperwork involved in managing a source safely and effectively, hopefully, we can also see why specialized software makes sense. Most of these records are essential. How they are completed and who is responsible for completing them, needs to be included in the agency's procedures for managing human sources and interlinked with the agency's procedures for managing intelligence. One does not work without the other. If an officer cannot be bothered to keep records properly, they are not suitable to manage sources and should be removed from the position. These records are needed to protect everyone involved. It does place an additional burden on those managing sources but given the risks involved, there is no other option.

4. Understanding Memory

We never know the whole truth about the past.

Niccolò Machiavelli (1469 -1527)

Introduction

In this chapter, we are going to take a brief look at the nature of memory. In simple terms, the primary reason that we manage sources is to get information from them. That information comes in one form or another from their memories. Predominantly, it will come directly from their memories of what they saw or heard, but it will also come from what they thought about what they saw and heard. But even in this latter case, what their thoughts were on the topic are constructed from previous memories of similar circumstances, with the same people. Even when we are asking a source to take on tasks for us in the future, the source is relying on their experience to know how to complete that task. That experience is held in their memory. As we can see all of what we are getting from a source is impacted by their memory.

In addition, the fact that the source has all these valuable memories stored in their brain does not mean that it is a simple job to access them. Let us consider the analogy of a bank. And let us assume that we know the bank has lots of money inside. Unless we know how to get that money out, it remains useless to us. The normal way we use is to go in and ask for the money, and assuming we have the right card with us, and we go at the right time, the bank is willing to give us a limited amount of that money. If we do not have the right card, we do not get anything. And if we want access to a lot more of the money, we are going to have to adopt a different approach. With a source, the traditional method of accessing the memories is to ask them. 'Who is selling drugs? Where do they sell them? What time do they sell them?' And if we are lucky, the source accesses the memories they have, and answers our questions. However, they give us an extremely limited amount of what they have stored in their memory. If we want more of those memories, we are going to have to adopt a different approach.

Furthermore, if we keep taking money out of a bank, and the bank does not keep restocking the money that they have, eventually the bank runs out of money. With a source, if they do not keep adding to their memory, eventually, after a period there will be nothing left in there that has utility for us. Their memory bank is bankrupted.

Staying with our banking analogy, we find that we have made one more assumption and that is that we know how to get the money out of the bank. Anyone that has gone to a bank in a foreign country may be familiar with what might happen. We use the same tactics we use at home. We go to the bank with our card, at the same time we go at home, only to find the bank does not open at those times or that we need our passport as well. We do not know how to access the money in *this* bank. It is the same with handling sources. We assume that Handlers know how to correctly access memories – all cops know how to ask questions. Everyone knows how to ask questions; it is easy. Actually, it's not, and as we will discuss asking questions is one of the last things we should be doing. And if all this was not problem enough, we assume that when the Handler gets the memory, they know how to keep it safe, in the same way, that when we get our money from the bank, we immediately put it in our wallet to keep it safe. Most Handlers, at best take limited measures to keep the memory safe, until it can be used in the way it should be.

Knowing how memories are constructed and retained, and how we can access those memories without damaging them as we access them, is essential knowledge for anyone involved in managing sources or the information they provide. If we don't see where potential errors can occur in the process, we cannot take measures to reduce or eliminate the risks involved. Many times we assume that a source is 'lying' when what has occurred is that what the source saw or heard, has been altered somewhere along the timeline of them seeing it and the Handler committing it to paper. Perhaps the source created a false memory, or perhaps the Handler distorted it as they accessed it, or as it was committed to an intelligence report, someone added to it, or detracted from it. If we want to understand how and why this happens, we need to understand memory.

A simple event

We are going to use a simple story to help illustrate points about memory. We are going to keep it relatively brief but with sufficient detail to illustrate several points. If it makes it easier for you to imagine, and there is a real benefit in this approach, change the characters to you being the source and meeting four friends at a local bar/restaurant that you have frequented.

The source, codename 'Atticus', and their four associates, Simon, Scott, Sharna, and Truck have gone out for a meal and a few drinks to the Red Herring sports bar. The event lasts two hours. They sat at the table beside the window. They have drinks and food.

[Unbeknownst to them, the entire event has been recorded with sound and video from numerous cameras around the bar.]

Your job as a Handler is to find out everything that happened at that event, from your source. And if what you get does not match exactly with what is on the video, either your source is lying or stupid, or you are lying or stupid. Which one is it? Because there is no way you have captured everything! We will now explore why. But before we do take a few minutes and try and pick out where the traps are in the story above. There are only 40 words so surely there cannot be that many traps! What are you not considering?

What is memory?

We don't need to be memory experts. A huge amount of research has been done about the nature of memory. From a practical perspective, there is a limited amount that the Handler needs to know to be more effective at their job. As we read through this, we should be thinking about the bar visit and how our source will have remembered the events. We will also make suggestions as to what the Handler may do during the debriefing of the source, or what they could have done before the event. We are continually trying to identify practical applications of the theory.

We will begin by looking at what we mean by the term memory. Memory is a function of the brain by which information is *encoded*, *stored*, and *retrieved* when needed (Melton,1963). We all tend to think of memory as being the storage bit and this is where a lot of errors occur. We need to understand all three elements. However, we will begin with how we can store memory and then return to the process of encoding and retrieving it.

Types of memory

Memory involves the retention of information over time, to influence our future actions. If things cannot be remembered, it is impossible for us to have language, to build relationships, or to have a sense of personal identity. We won't know how to do things or where we have left things of value, like our car keys, or our glasses, or our cell phone.

There are three categories of memory, short-term memory, long-term memory, and working memory. Short term memory can hold about five items for an extremely limited period, approximately one minute. This is only as long as nothing else is thrown at us at the same time. Try remembering five items if someone is talking, especially about something similar. For example, consider the license plate of a car that passes us. If we don't write it down by the time it goes out of view, we will have forgotten some of it. Short term memories are held in our conscious mind. We know they are there because we are working hard to keep them there. The best example of a short-term memory at work, is holding someone's telephone number in our brain, as we try and key it into our phone. With the length of numbers now we can't do it, so we have to split them up into smaller batches or chunks.

The 'long term' memory is where a person stores information over a prolonged period arguably for a lifetime. The capacity of long-term memory is all but limitless. We can, and do, store a lifetime of memories. There are two types of long-term memory, *implicit* and *explicit*. Implicit memories are stored in a way that allows us to remember them without having to make any effort. For this reason, implicit memory is sometimes referred to as unconscious memory or automatic memory. Implicit memory is associated with motor skills. It allows us to perform everyday physical activities, such as walking, driving a car, or riding a bike. We do these without any conscious thought.

154

When we drive home from work and we can't remember the drive, that is implicit memory at work. We have done it so often our brain just runs seemingly on automatic pilot. We do what we have to do without thinking. We can also see implicit memory at play when we watch someone who has repeatedly trained to develop a skill, such as a musician. Everything they do seems so easy for them. They sit at the keys of a piano and their fingers move as if by magic. Similarly, with soldiers who have trained and trained, until their skills are so ingrained that when they are in a combat situation fear does not impede their behavior. Their implicit memory automatically tells their body what to do.

On the other hand, explicit memory requires conscious effort to access the things we want to remember. We need to think about what we are doing. When it comes to managing sources and indeed to the interviewing of any witness or suspect, it is explicit memory that is of most significance to us. Explicit memory can further be divided into two separate but interlinked parts, semantic memory, and episodic memory. Both are important and it is easy to confuse the two, from a theoretical perspective but more importantly, from a practical perspective, especially when debriefing a source.

Episodic and semantic memory.

Explicit memory can be further divided into two further parts, *semantic memory*, and e*pisodic memory*

(Tulving and Thomson 1972). Understanding the difference is critical when it comes to effectively debriefing a source. Semantic memory refers to the general knowledge that we accumulate throughout our lives. It includes basic facts like the names of colors, the sounds of letters, the types of animals, and the understanding of language. Semantic memory is how we store facts in isolation and as part of wider interrelated groupings, into which we place these isolated facts. Brown goes into the color box and a dog goes into the animal box. A brown dog will be linked to both things that are brown, and to animals. We will also put people into groups. Some may go into the box for friends while others go into the box related to work.

Episodic memory is the collection of past personal experiences that occurred at a particular time and place. It is how we remember specific events or *episodes*. Episodic memory is specific to the individual. It is about their interpretation of what occurred. It is their memory of their experiences and of specific events in time. Episodic memory is used for personal memories, such as the sensations, emotions, and personal associations of a particular place or time. Episodic memories are contextually embedded. We cannot separate the memory from the context in which it was created. (We will return to this later.) From these memories, people can reconstruct the actual events that took place at a specific time in their lives. An easy way to think of this is to think of episodes in a season of a Netflix drama. Different things happen in each episode that come together to form a story. A word of caution here. We all know how difficult it is to sort out

156

what happened in each episode after we have watched the final installment. How many of us say: 'I knew that was going to happen!' A source's life is made up of numerous episodes. If we leave it too long between meetings, we get a summary of what has happened but with a lot of detail left out. We want all the detail.

Depending on how memories are retrieved there is potential for the semantic memory to either enhance or corrupt the retrieval of episodic memory. For example, a person who witnesses a shooting on their regular journey to their place of worship, on a Sunday morning will potentially contaminate their account of the shooting, with memories of what happens every other Sunday. These will have been drawn from their semantic memory, the box[9] that holds 'Sunday go to church memories.' The techniques we use to retrieve memories of the shooting, may either reduce or exacerbate this problem.

When analyzing how a source will obtain memories of events we need to realize that they will likely be stored in both semantic and episodic memory. Much of what the source reports on will form part of their daily routine. This means that when the source is recalling specific events that are of interest to the Handler, they may be contaminated with semantic memories. For

---

[9] Memories are not actually stored in boxes. It is a lot more complicated. However, the analogy of a box may help understanding that one type of memories is separated from other types of memories. It is worth bearing in mind that each box may be further subdivided. This the animal box will have subsections for types of dogs, types of cat, etc.

example, if our source works as a car mechanic in a workshop, he may have been visited by an associate on a particular day. If we are not careful in how we debrief the source they are likely to get memories of the visit, mixed up with what is normally happening at the workshop. The conversation may go like this:

'What day did Frank come?
Tuesday.
Where you alone?
No. Bill was there. He was working in the tire bay.
Did he hear what was said?
Wait…Bill took a half-day last Tuesday.'

Bill is normally present and normally works in the tire bay. The source initially merges semantic and episodic memories. Often this will go undetected. The question/answer format is flawed. Furthermore, many inexperienced Handlers will jump to the conclusion that the source is being deceptive.

Considering our story at the Red Herring bar, there is a real risk that if this is a regular haunt for this group, what happened there on that night may be contaminated with memories of what usually happens there. For example, they may always order nachos and beer, but on this particular occasion, Simon was drinking a soft drink. This may be an indication he had something else happening afterward. Small details missed can have a significant impact. Furthermore. they can open a path to other memories:

'Hold on. Simon wasn't drinking. He said something about having to pick up something later. He had a two-hour drive ahead of him. It is not like him, not to have any beer. It must have been important.'

Handlers will continually be debriefing episodes in the source's life. There will always be significant overlaps from one episode to the next. For example, Atticus may have been with these four associates on Tuesday night. On Wednesday, he may have spent the day with Simon, and on Friday, he may have met Sharna at the football game. Saturday night was spent back in the Red Herring with Simon, Scott, and two others. As Handlers, we need to find out what happened at each of these episodes.

Working Memory

The third type of memory we will discuss is what is known as working memory. This is often used interchangeably with short-term memory but there are significant differences. Working memory refers not only to the retention of information but also the simultaneous usage of that information. It is about the amount of information we can hold in our mind at any one time, while at the same time we are trying to use those pieces of information. As a general rule we can hold up to about seven pieces of information, and then something is lost. One way of thinking about working memory is to consider the changing room at a clothes store. The clothes store has thousands of pieces of clothing in-store, but we are only allowed to take a maximum of seven items into the dressing room at any one time. If we want the eighth item, we have to leave it with the assistant until we return one of the other pieces. Over a period, we can bring in an unlimited number of items, but only retain seven at any one time. It is similar with working memory. What we are doing is bringing different items from in-store i.e. our long-term memory and considering them. If we want another one, we have to give one back. We do not even realize we are doing it and we often can't remember what we have just 'forgotten' i.e. returned to our long-term memory. And as we will see, what we have returned, is not the same as we brought in.

The way that we cope with limited working memory is to get the ideas down on paper. When we are trying to see what is occurring with the source or with the criminal gang, we need to write what we know down. We simply do not have the mental capacity to hold it all in our working memory. This is particularly relevant if we are having a team meeting about the source. Team members will be putting forward different facts and ideas. We need to write them down in some simplified form that shows the main elements of the problem and how they relate to each other. Unless we are capturing them contemporaneously, some of them will be lost. For example, if we are looking at whether or not we should use a source in an operation we may think first about the arguments in favor of deploying the source. Then, we will hear the arguments against deploying the source. And then we have overloaded our working memory. We cannot keep all those pros and cons in our heads, at the same time, and see how they play off against each other. Inevitably, this leads to bad decisions being made generally with who shouted loudest or last, winning the argument. Only by using external memory aids are we able to cope with the volume and complexity of the information we will need to use. Analysts can assist greatly with this process because they have the tools to present the information being discussed, in many different formats.

Having a better understanding of the different ways we store our memories, allows us to better understand some of the challenges involved in accessing those memories at a later time. The ways we store a memory are summarised in Figure 4.1

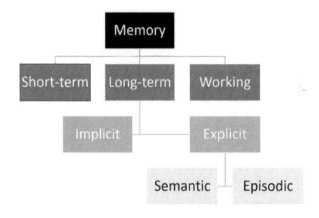

Figure 4.1 Types of Memory

Now that we know the different types of storage available to us for storing memories, lets us return to the process of how information is encoded, stored, and retrieved, when needed.

Encoding

Encoding is the first step to creating a new memory. It allows the perceived item of interest to be converted into a construct, that can be stored within our brain indefinitely. Our memories are a personal account. What we later recall is our experience of the event. This is not necessarily the same as the event. When we witness an event first-hand, we do not take in everything that has occurred, and what enters may vary in trace strength. The quality of memory will vary.

The process of encoding begins with attention. For information to be encoded we must first pay attention to it. The process of paying attention to a particular piece of information is called attentional capture. By paying attention to a particular piece of information, whilst excluding other concurrent pieces of information, we create memories that are unique to us. This is why two people see the same situation but create different memories about it. This way when a source tells us what happened at an event, we must realize it is their view, their memory, of that event. We must make accommodations for that. All too often we put it down to deceit or incompetence on their part. We all perform attentional capture differently. There are two main types of attentional capture: explicit and implicit.

162

Explicit attentional capture is when something becomes salient enough that we want to attend to it. We become aware of its existence, and something about its nature, motivates us to pay greater attention to it. For example, we may be in the middle of fixing something, then a news article comes on television about our town. Our attention is drawn to it and we stop what we are doing, so we can find out exactly what has happened. This has relevance with sources. If we direct a source to pay attention to particular matters beforehand, they are more likely to attend to them if and when they occur. They are primed to attend to what we want. Think about our story: If we had told our source to attend to everything Scott says, how much more likely are they to obtain more detail about him?

Implicit attentional capture occurs when something that we may not even be consciously aware of has an impact on our mental performance. We all know how difficult it is to learn things if there is a lot of noise going on around us. If we are trying to remember details and someone in the background is tapping on a bench, while we may not consciously take it under notice, are attention will be impacted. Again, we need to think about the difficulties that the source may have had to deal with, as they tried to remember what we have asked them to remember. Think about our story: How much background noise is there in a bar? How difficult will it be to hear let alone remember everything?

Emotion tends to increase attention, and the more

emotional the event is the more vividly it will be stored, and the more readily we will be able to retrieve it. Unfortunately, it doesn't mean that we will be able to retrieve it any more accurately. High levels of emotional arousal also lead to attention narrowing. The piece of the event that is central to the source's emotional arousal will be attended to more strongly, while peripheral details will be missed. Here again, we have to think about a source working in an environment where there is a high level of risk to their safety. If they are concentrating on that, it stands to reason that a lot of what is going on around them will be missed. A source may not remember the type of gun that was present if they are concentrating on the face of the person, they think they might be about to use it. The Handler may think: 'He had a gun pointed at you. You must remember if it was a pistol or revolver.' The source may say 'I have no fucking idea but his eyes are blue.' The source's attention was on the person's face to identify what they may do.

The next part of encoding is perception. This involves the identification, organization, and interpretation of information from our senses, within the context in which it is occurring. All five senses may be used in the encoding. This is why we remember smells, sounds, etc, and associate those sounds and smells with a particular memory. The creation of mental pictures is one way we visually encode memories. We may implant memories related to sound by saying something over and over again and creating an audio memory of the event. Information that we perceive directly, with our ears or see with our eyes, is likely to be remembered

164

better than something we have heard second-hand. During encoding our brain takes the new information as we perceive it, and connects this information, to things that we already know. Our brain analyses everything coming from our senses and decides what will be committed to long-term memory. New material is connected to old material and then stored in different parts of our brain. Our memories are *constructed* by and will be affected by, how we understood the event, both consciously and unconsciously. The characteristics of the environment are encoded as part of the memory of the event. This is similar to the metadata that is stored when we take a digital photograph or create a computer document. We will discuss later how this contextual data can be used to aid the retrieval of a memory (context reinstatement). As the memory is encoded the more associations that are made with existing memories the more likely it is to be remembered

The encoding processing involves making judgments about the meaning of the new information, its relevance to us, and the mental activity that is needed to integrate the material we deem relevant, into our long-term memory. Not all information we have sensed is encoded equally well. To use the computer analogy again, sometimes we think we have saved changes and we have not. Sometimes, for whatever reason, there is only a partial save. Sometimes we accidentally overwrite what we wanted to save. Sometimes we know we saved it, but we do not know where we saved it to, so we can't find it when we need it. Our memory is a bit like that, only much worse.

Storage

As we have discussed, the second phase is that of the memory being stored. We committed the thing or event, to our long-term memory. In the process of it being stored, we also store the connections that link the separate pieces of the memory together. For example, Americans of a certain generation will remember where they were and what they were doing, when they heard John F Kennedy had been assassinated. The event, the assassination may be remembered along with something relatively unimportant like, I was making coffee, or, I was just out of the shower. These circumstances under which we learn new information are relevant when we try to recall that information later. They are interconnected with and can provide a pathway to, the memory.

Connected to the memory will be the emotions we were feeling at the time it was created. These are stored as part of the memory. These also create a path to obtaining greater detail on retrieval. The memory will also be connected to things that objectively speaking, it should not be connected to, but for that person, the brain made a connection. During the storage process, we will have associated memories with the new material because there seemed, to our brain, to be a connection. Objectively, there was not, or perhaps there was a tenuous connection. Most of us will have been in an argument where the other party seems to be dragging up the past. Their brain is making links with previous events and tying the present situation, to those memories. For them, everything seems connected, while for us it may seem we are arguing about totally different things. Similarly, we have all been in the middle of a conversation when the other person comes out with what appears to be a completely random and unconnected thought. What is occurring here, is that their brain is processing through memories and it has found links to the present conversation, and this apparently random thought. For them it is connected but we may reply dismissively: 'Where did that come from?' Because the links were made in the unconscious mind the person cannot explain and becomes embarrassed. In source situations, the Handler should not be dismissive. There is a connection between the current topic and what the source has said. It may be important. Explore it with the source.

Some factors will impact what is stored and how well it is stored. The duration of the exposure to the event is critical. If it was fleeting, then it is likely there will be little detail remembered. Similarly, with the frequency of exposure, the more often we see something the more likely we are to remember it. For example, if we encounter a new word, we need to see it about five times before we remember it well enough to use it comfortably. However, sometimes if we see something often, we fail to pay attention to the details. This is why we don't notice when our partner has got their hair styled. What was happening around us at the time the memory was being stored, will have an impact. Things like the amount of noise, how clear the visibility was, and any other distractions will play a part. The seriousness of the event will play a big part. Most people can count easily on one hand the number of life-changing events they have encountered. The salience of the event to the person will be relevant, particularly if there is a threat to the person's safety or well-being. If we have been exposed to some form of threat, we will remember it. If an event is predictable, we may not pay as much attention to it. However, in the source world, we can predict many of the things that are likely to happen. This benefits us because we can direct the source to pay attention to it. If an event surprises us, naturally we will attend to it. We need, to make sure we are safe. If our attention is divided between and several factors, then it is more difficult to store memories about each of the contemporaneous events. Think of our story where the source is at the meeting with his four associates. Potentially two or three conversations are going on simultaneously. Which one should the source attend to? Another thing to consider is that remembering things is hard work. We have to expend effort to do it. Generally speaking, we remember the minimum amount that is necessary for our benefit. Why waste energy remembering unnecessary things? Handlers have to motivate the source to put the effort in.

Another factor that will always be relevant is the psychological make-up of the source. Sources come in many different varieties. Many of them, like the rest of us, have 'issues'. Some may have underlying mental health issues such as a personality disorder. A person with a personality disorder thinks, feels, and relates to others very differently from the average person. Furthermore, sources are likely to have varying degrees of intellectual ability and emotional intelligence. These will affect their ability to obtain and retain information. We must get to know the capabilities of our source and be realistic about what they can achieve. There is little point in creating conflict with a source for not remembering something, if they simply do not have the mental capacity to remember it. This is bad handling. Another comment fault is for a Handler to underestimate the ability of a source. This often stems from the Handler's shortcomings. They look down on the source because of the way the source speaks, or their background, and they miss how 'smart' the source is. A key attribute of a Handler is to see past stereotypical views and see the reality. Notwithstanding this, some people may want to be a source but because of their lifestyle, they are not suitable to be a source. If for example Atticus, went to the Red herring and got so drunk they could not stand up, their memories will not be accurate no matter how much they insist that they are. Similarly, if they are addicted to drugs their memories will always be suspect. These factors should be highlighted in the risk documents and will be a factor in grading all subsequent intelligence reports.

Perhaps the biggest risk to the accurate storage of memory is post-event information. A memory is created at a moment in time, if we do not access it very shortly after, inevitably it will be changed. We will learn new things and we will link the new things to the old memory creating an amalgam of the old and new. There is a huge risk of the source's memory of an event being corrupted, if we do not meet with them as soon as practically possible, after that event. Consider what will happen if our source Atticus, meets with Sharna two days after the meal, and they revisit what happened at the Red Herring bar. The source's memories of what occurred that night will be changed. This can cause major inconsistencies in their reporting.

Memories are constructed together with all the associated links. At a certain point in time, we can say that a memory has been constructed. It does not remain static. Over time it will fade. Some details will become vague while others, that have more relevance for the person, emerge with greater clarity. Perhaps the person reminisces on them. Perhaps they have greater salience at that time in the person's life. We have all ruminated over something that was said to us, or something that happened to us, playing it over and over again in our mind. And each time we do we change the construction, unconsciously adding bits to it while changing other aspects. We take the memory out, play it over, then put it back with newer information added to it, yet we are certain that what we remember is exactly as it happened, at the time. With each reconstruction greater distortion occurs. We want to capture that memory in its purest form. We need to meet sources regularly. When things are critical, we may want our source to contact us immediately after a meeting.

Other considerations that the Handler must be aware of, relate to the source as an individual, and the circumstances during which some memories are acquired. For example, how long they were exposed to the event, what was their view of it and where there may have been impediments to remembering the event. Sources are very often under considerable stress. During a specific event, because of their role in it, the pressure on them may have increased. This will affect the quality of memory and the extent to which it does, comes down to the individual. For example, a source may witness his associates take someone around a corner into an alley to assault them. There is likely to be a lot of stress, a limited view of events and it may all happen very quickly. However, the Handler's perspective is likely to be: 'You were there you must know everything that happened.'

Let us now take a brief look at how our source Atticus, may have stored the memories of the meeting at the Red Herring Bar. They are likely to have linked all the people together. If they talked about buildings or houses, they will be linked together. There may have been a conversation around Sharna's family circumstances, which then lead to revelations about her child and her use of drugs. Scott was driving and he went out to the car to bring in a bag for Truck, from which he brought out a cell phone. The source does not know who Truck is. That is only his nickname. He was brought to the meeting by Simon. Truck is involved in laundering money and transporting drugs. And Simon's nickname is Tiger. This is a snapshot of how this may all look in our source's brain. Now double it and multiply it by infinity, and you may have an idea of how it really looks.

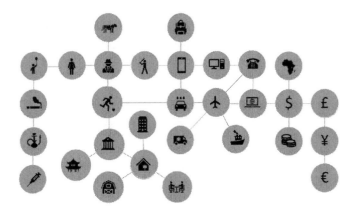

Figure 4.2 The Memories of Atticus

Hopefully, after this discussion, we can recognize the difficulties in storing memories and the limitations of our memory. Consider the Handler who believes they can have an hour-long conversation with a source and remember everything that was said. At best, they will remember partial details, about the bits that were most salient for them. In reality, they will have forgotten most of what the source has said and distorted quite a bit of the rest. We forget how quickly we forget.

Retrieval

The third element in our definition of memory, coming after encoding and storage, is retrieval. We need to be able to get at the information we have previously stored. And we need to be able to get it out when we need that information. In a source relationship, it is the responsibility of the Handler to get the information that the source is storing. Before going any further about the retrieval process, we need to acknowledge that there are several differences regarding extracting memories from a source and recalling something for our *own* benefit. Furthermore, in the law enforcement context, there are significant differences in extracting memories from a witness than from a source.

When we want to remember something, for our benefit, there is no danger in recalling it. For a source, they may want to keep some things hidden from the Handler, so they are continuously choosing what to talk about, and what to omit. If we imagine a memory as a bag of M and Ms, the source is deciding what the Handler is getting; they can have the red one but not the yellow one, the blue one but not the green one, and they can have a bit of the salted caramel one just to get them interested.

Debriefing a source is not the same as interviewing a witness. Normally, a witness is providing information about one event[10] of which they had no prior warning. With a witness there is limited potential for the cross-contamination of the memories associated with one event and those with other similar events. Most times when we are debriefing a source, we will want the source to talk about many events. There is much greater potential for cross-contamination. Furthermore, there will be an ongoing relationship

---

[10] It is recognised that some witnesses, such as victims of repeated sexual abuse or victims of domestic violence, do have to recall multiple events.

173

with the source, they will know what is expected. With a witness it is a one-time occurrence; everything about the retrieval process will be new and have to be explained.

For the moment we will look at the process of how memory retrieval normally works. For example, we will think about how we would recount to a friend an event at the office, or how we access the memory of who are classmates were at high school or where we may have left our car keys. Later we will look at all the problems in getting access to the source's memories.

We retrieve our memories from our long-term memory. If someone asks me 'What is the capital of Germany?' I go into my semantic memory. I take the path to the box for countries, then I follow the link to the subsection on capitals and there it is 'Bonn.' Actually, it is not. It was when I first learned it and the memory is still there. I see there is another link and when I go down that path, I see that the capital is now Berlin. It changed with the reunification of Germany. And from there I can see paths leading to boxes that will hold details of how the reunification came about. Then to the 2nd World War, etc. I will also see a path leading to the movie box and in it is one of my favorite movies, The Lives of Others, a movie about East Berlin, during the Cold War. And so it continues... This is a typical example of how we remember things. It starts with a simple question, but all our memories are linked, one thing leads to another. That's why in my brain at the moment, instead of thinking about what I am writing, I am remembering backpacking through

174

Germany, before Germany was reunited. And all because of a simple question! The learning point here is that, when we are talking to a source, we rarely want to interrupt these 'ramblings' because we do not know where they will take us. There is little that the source can tell us, that we do not want to know.

As we can see from this example accessing memories from long-term memory can be a laborious process. Tulving (1991) describes memory as a network of associations, with different ways to access it. We need to go into the network and find the paths that will take us to where we want to go. Consider the network in the memories of Atticus as laid out in Figure 4.2 If we want to find out about money-laundering, we can see there are many potential pathways to start that journey, but also many ways we can be sidetracked.

Retrievability is influenced by the number of locations in which information is stored and the number and strength of pathways from this information to these locations. The more frequently a path is followed, the stronger that path becomes and the more readily available is the information located along that path. If we have not thought of a subject for some time, it may be difficult to recall details. However, we can get past a block by considering several potential routes to that information. For example, if I can't find my car keys then I will activate my memory like this. 'When did I last have them? This evening. I had to unlock the apartment door. I came in. They are not in my jacket pocket. I brought the bag of food into the kitchen…There they are, on the worktop.' After

175

putting ourselves back into context in which the event occurred it is easier to find the general location in our memory, and the opportunities for greater recall become more readily available. We begin to remember names, places, and events that had seemed to be forgotten. Once we have started thinking about a problem in one-way, other mental circuits, or pathways, get activated. These get strengthened each time we think about the memory. This facilitates the easier retrieval of the memory at a later time.

Memories are context dependant. We can remember things better if the context is the same as when we recalled them. When I am trying to remember where I put my keys, I put myself back to yesterday evening, I think about opening my door, I think about being glad to get home from work, I think about how hungry I was feeling. I remember having the food with me. I remember taking it into the kitchen. The keys are there.

If we want to remember what happened at a particular place, we start with *context reinstatement*. We put ourselves back in the place at the time of the event. We try and remember everything about it, the smells, the sounds, everyone that was present, and everything that was going on. Later we will talk about using this knowledge to enable the source to better recall what has occurred.

The retrieval of memory is not perfect. This means that while a memory may exist, it will not always be possible to bring that memory back in its original form – there is always the potential for distortion. Knowledge of the

176

nuances of retrieval is beneficial to the Handler in several ways. Firstly, Handlers are often suspicious that a source is not telling everything that lies within their knowledge. It may be that the source simply can't remember it. Secondly, the source may remember some aspects of an event in great detail and others in less detail. Understanding may help avoid unnecessary conflict. Third, after a noticeably short period, about an hour, we forget significant details. This initial memory loss is compounded by a slower but further degradation of the memory, over the days following the event. Fourth, memories can become corrupted over time. The significance here is that the greater time that elapses between a source observing an event and the Handler debriefing the source about that event, escalates the potential for loss off or corruption to the memory, when it is eventually retrieved. The tendency in source management is often to reduce meetings to as few as possible, but this may exacerbate the problem of memories being corrupted.

There are many other aspects of memory retrieval that are of interest. We all like to tell a story with us at the center of it and we all want to look good in the story. We block out what is not relevant for us, or what makes us look bad. We do this consciously and unconsciously. The source will do the same. They will always be careful about how they appear to the Handler. Poor questioning will lead to poor answers and will potentially corrupt the memory. This is why interviewing a person again in the proper way after someone else has done it badly, may not achieve success. Finally, existing memories will automatically influence the encoding of later events.

Without going into the how and why of it, the Handler needs to recognize that the source will recall events that they believe happened but never happened. They will add detail to a story that was never there. They will change their story from one telling, to the next telling. And these all happen even when the source is willing to remember what we ask them to remember, and to tell us everything when we ask them to tell us.

The Handler needs to train the source not to omit anything during the debrief regardless of how irrelevant it may seem to them, or how damaging it may be to them. The source needs to know that omitting details may expose the source to risk. Only by telling everything can they be fully protected. The primary motive for the source to be truthful will always be their safety.

Going forward

As we have said, one way we can get more information is for the Handler to highlight to the source the nature of events that the Handler wishes the source to attend to. In many circumstances, a Handler will be able to predict the type of event the source is likely to encounter, and task them accordingly. As the relationship between Handler and source progresses, the source will learn what is expected from them and their behavior will change. This will happen provided

178

the Handler is consistent in their demands and in the way in which they debrief the source. If the source knows they will be asked for details, they are much more likely to get the details. With good handling, it gets to the stage where the source is giving over details without even being asked for them. They know their role; they know what they are expected to remember.

Sometimes it can be useful to teach the source simple mnemonics that, over time, help them remember greater detail. These are shown in Table 4.1. They are for the most part self-explanatory. In vehicles, peculiarities refer to anything distinguishing about the car such as a different colored door, or a sticker on the rear. In relation to people distinguishing features will include things like an unusual hairstyle, a scar, or a tattoo. An accent or speech impediment would also be included here. Gait and posture refer to how the person walks or sits. He may have a limp or sit in a hunched up way. Considering if the person was holding anything can help trigger other memories. Perhaps they had a sports bag or car keys. All these things help identify the vehicle or person at a later time. They are also particularly useful for anyone who is carrying out surveillance on the person. The greater detail, the more opportunities exist to trigger other memories. We are also subtly training the source to be more observant.

VEHICLES T C N P		PEOPLE A to H	
T	Type	**A**	Age
C	Colour	**B**	Build
N	Number	**C**	Clothes
P	Peculiarities	**D**	Distinguishing features
		E	Ethnicity
		F	Face
		G	Gait and Posture
		H	Holding

Table 4.1 Mnemonics

The Red Herring

Let us go back to our visit to the Red Herring with our 5 people. What we are trying to do with this story is to apply our new knowledge of the nature of memory to a situation, in which a source will often find themselves. The Handler should begin to see how the memories may have been created in the mind of Atticus, and be thinking about how they would go about extracting these memories. We will first consider some examples of what the cameras recorded and try and predict some of the difficulties the source will have in recounting events. (Table 4.2)

CAMERAS	SOURCE
Simon and Sharna were already seated when Atticus arrived.	What conversation took place before the source's arrival?
Scott arrived at the meeting in a red Ford Pickup with Truck	The source was inside at the time and could not see the car.
Scott and Simon left the table for ten minutes and sat at another table.	The source will have seen this but not heard it.
Sharna had a long conversation near the bar with one of the waiters.	Will the source have any idea what it was about?
Atticus went to the restrooms. He was absent from the table for about six minutes.	What would the source have missed in this time?

Table 4.2 Camera/Source Comparison

These are just a few examples of how our expectation of what a source should know differs from what they actually know. We can see in these examples, how much has potentially been missed.

Now let us look at some things the cameras did not see but that Atticus may be able to help us with. Atticus may be able to explain why Simon and Sharna were there before the others. 'Simon has the hots for her. He never misses a chance to get her on her own'. Atticus may know a lot about Scott's Ford pickup. 'He drives a red pickup. He has had it for years. It was his Father's. His Father's dead…' Atticus may know that the waiter that Sharna spoke to is her cousin and that the cousin is not involved in anything.

Simon and Truck had a private conversation while at the table. Unless we previously told Atticus to attend specifically to Simon this detail may be lost. Atticus may vaguely remember that they spoke together for ten minutes but we will get nothing of the content. If Atticus had been directed to prioritize information on Simon they may have heard or seen more. This is how giving the source-specific taskings can enhance the quality of information they collect.

There is a risk in the source taking notes. While it may aid their memory, if they are caught with them, they will be in trouble. If the Handler thinks the source can safely make notes, then they need to train them on how to do it safely. The trip Atticus made to the bathroom allowed him to make a note about something important he had heard.

Conclusion

Memory is not a movie of yesterday, never changing as it is streamed, time and time again. Memory is like an oak tree, changing with seasons, growing and continually evolving. What was there yesterday may have been lost, what is here today, has grown upon what was there yesterday, and what is there tomorrow may be something we do not recognize.

5. Cognitive Debriefing

It is a capital mistake to theorize before one has data.
Insensibly one begins to twist facts to suit theories, instead
of theories to suit facts.

A Scandal in Bohemia - Sir Arthur Conan Doyle

Introduction

Now that we have structures in place and we have a better understanding of the nature of memory, we are going to discuss the process of extracting the information that the source has in their head. We refer to this as carrying out a source debrief or ***debriefing***. Source debriefing is defined as:

the process of obtaining information from a source and
delivering instruction to that source in a way designed to
maximize the quality and quantity of information
obtained.

Debriefing a source is not about the passive receipt of information, it involves many different aspects. First, it is about gaining the maximum about of information. Second, we want to ensure the quality of that information in terms of both its veracity and detail. Third, source debriefs are both retrospective and prospective in nature. They seek to obtain information about what has occurred in the past and also seek to obtain information about intentions, plans, and possible future events. Fourth, source debriefs involve tasking the source. We do not send the source out hoping they will get information. We direct them as to the type of information we want. We tell them what tasks we want them to do. We discuss with them their concerns and capabilities around these tasks, and we train them on how to do them. Source debriefing is complex. There are many different things for the Handlers to consider and it involves using many different techniques.

Debriefing sources can be carried out in different ways, with the method of debriefing having to be adapted to meet the personal circumstances of the source. Each debrief has to be carried out balancing the security of the source with the demands of the agency, all while maintaining a healthy relationship with that source and meeting their needs. We discussed the competing needs in Chapter 1 and in no situation are they more likely to conflict than during a debrief. Both Handlers and sources will be concerned for their safety. The Handlers will want to maximize the amount of information while having to comply with procedures, and the source will want whatever they want, from the meeting and the relationship in general.

Figure 5.1 Competing needs (repeated)

One of the problems we are likely to encounter in suggesting a new method of debriefing sources is that officers have been using the old methods for many years and they have had success with these methods. For them, there seems little incentive to change. The method employed is a question and answer format. The Handler asks a question and the source answers it. Unfortunately, because Handlers have often not been trained into how to ask good questions, they continue to ask the type of question that limits the source's ability to reply accurately. 'Did you see Tom this week?' This is a closed question. It allows for only two possible answers: Yes or No. A better question would be: Who have you seen this week? But this assumes the source has seen anyone. They feel pressure to talk about someone.

To compound the problem many of the interviewing techniques that continue to be taught to police have serious flaws. Some are coercive, seeking only to get admissions as opposed to the facts, while others over-simplify the theoretical knowledge, so it all fits into an easily remembered mnemonic, for example, the PEACE model. Both these attitudes can be summed up in the statements: 'All cops want is a confession'. and 'They are so dumb we need to keep everything simple for them.' Despite all the new knowledge we have about how the human brain works; many officers still rely on methods that were developed in the 1940s and use the good cop/bad cop format.

This chapter takes the best practices that have been created operationally over many years, adds structure to the process, and integrates those interviewing techniques which have been researched and validated as being the most likely to recover the maximum amount of accurate information. Furthermore, it takes cognizance of all the other factors at play in a source relationship. This chapter is not about law enforcement interviewing, it is about debriefing a human source. There is a crossover, but the two things are not the same.

Debriefing locations

A debriefing may take place in many ways including physical meetings, telephone contact, or internet communication. All of these will have an impact on our ability to debrief the source and the methods we choose to use. We will summarise some of the options together with some of the pros and cons. However, what must be born in mind is that there are also a significant number of considerations that fall under the topic of fieldcraft, and that impact on how and where debriefs take place.

A common method of obtaining information from a source is a telephone debrief. Telephone debriefs are a useful way of cutting down on the number of physical meetings. They help maintain the relationship and provide for timely information. Sometimes telephone contact may be the only means available to get the information when it is needed. They are a standard way of operating for the majority of Handlers. The logistics of physical meetings including security concerns, mean that telephone debriefs are an easy way of maintaining regular contact with a source. Information is obtained quickly from the source, thus reducing the potential for the source's memory being corrupted, between the time they receive it and they are in a position to have a physical meet with the Handler. The problems with telephone debriefing include the fact that the Handler misses all the attendant non-verbal communication that would be available in a physical meet, and the very nature of telephone calls is time-limiting. There is insufficient time to obtain or fully examine, the information provided. There are also risks that the circumstances in which the source makes any telephone call are likely to remain unknown to the Handler. Furthermore, because telephone debriefs are a much easier form of regular contact than physical meetings there is a temptation for both source and Handler to place an over-reliance on them with the result that the relationship is neglected. In all aspects of telephone contact, there is a risk of calls being overheard or intercepted. There is also a risk of compromise through telephone billing records or electronic data retention.

Another method of debriefing that is becoming increasingly common is using emails or texting. In the truest sense of the definition, the use of emails or any of the many electronic messaging apps to provide the Handler with information does not fall within our definition of debriefing. This method is merely the passive receipt of information. Whilst on some occasions it has utility, there is no opportunity to clarify any of the information, or to add to it. Also, it does nothing to sustain or develop the relationship. At best it is a stop-gap. And because we are all lazy, and we are now so used to doing this with our personal relationships, it becomes our method of choice with sources. These methods for obtaining information from a source should only be used where there is no alternative and they are no substitute for face-to-face contact. Where a controller identifies that this is what is occurring, they should question why it is occurring and if it is the choice of the source or Handler. Either way, there is a problem.

When most Handlers talk about debriefing a source, they mean an unstructured, face-to-face meeting. Unstructured here infers a lack of a plan about what will occur. The total extent of planning will look something like this: 'We will meet at Joe's café. We will get a coffee[11] and we will ask him what is new. And if we remember we will ask him if he has anything more on what he told us last time. Then we will give him his money and off we will all go.[12] And these meetings will take place in a variety of places including cafes, bars, or hotel rooms. We may also use a vehicle and if we do, we may choose to collect the source and park up somewhere, or just keep driving. With all these meeting locations there are pros and cons. There should be an ongoing discussion between Handlers and the Controller to decide which is the best place to meet under a given set of circumstances, and then with the source to ensure, the proposal suits them. There will always be a need for compromise. Face-to-face meetings are the best kind of debriefing, but they need planning.

Time

One factor that will always play a part in source debriefing is time. One of the reasons we have Dedicated Source Units is so that the Handlers will have the necessary time available to manage sources safely and effectively. They are not having to balance their duties with the source against other things, like investigations or file preparation. They are not having to explain to a manager who neither understands nor cares why they need to spend time with a source who

---

[11] And a donut!

[12] Well we might stay for another coffee. No point in rushing back to the office.

is having problems. Handler time is devoted exclusively to the management of sources. It is not the same for a source. Every minute they spend with the Handler is a stolen moment. It is a moment in which they may have to account to someone else as to where they have been, and one which they cannot account for. In addition, the source may have to invest time in obtaining information for the Handler. This time is stolen from their family or their workplace. Again, it is time that is difficult for them to account for. When deciding what type of debrief should be conducted, time will always be a key factor. There will rarely be enough time. Maximizing the use of the time that is available, is one reason to have a structure for debriefs.

Interviewing versus debriefing - identifying the differences

It is acknowledged that there is a lack of empirical evidence to identify the problems that exist in source debriefing. However, it is relatively safe to make the judgment that it is highly likely to be similar to what occurs in other aspects of police interviewing, where significant research has been carried out. Much of the existing research points to a deficit in both listening and questioning skills. For example, research by Fisher, Geiselman, and Raymond (1987) identified specific problems, including repeated interruptions by officers, poor sequencing of questions, inappropriate question types, and poor wording of questions. If these types of problems are occurring in ordinary police interviews, then it is highly likely they are at play with sources.

Furthermore, anecdotal evidence provided by Handlers gives a clear indication of a lack of structure concerning the task. Many will openly admit that they have had extremely limited, if any training, about how to debrief a source.

There are some key differences between the interviewing of a witness, a victim, or a suspect, and that of debriefing a source. However, there are many also similarities. At times, a source will have witnessed events. At other times, they will have been involved in the perpetration of some of the events which they are describing. On occasions, they may have been the victim in the event on which they are reporting, but unwilling to make any formal complaint. What we end up with is a paradox where a source can be all these things, while at the same time none of them.

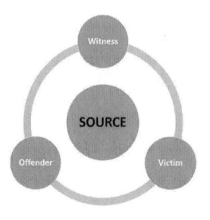

Figure 5.2 Source Offender Victim Witness Paradox

Before looking at the differences between law enforcement interviewing and source debriefing it is recognized that there is considerable scientific-based evidence available to support the suggested techniques that work in getting a person to recall memories. We do know what techniques are most likely to get an accurate recall in interviews. We may not use them, but the knowledge is there. These techniques are still valid in the debriefing context but what we have to do is examine that context, and see what adaptations we may need to make, to increase their utility. So, what are the contextual differences?

There are some fundamental differences apparent when contrasting the interview of a witness and the debrief of a source. First, there is the presence of an already existing relationship between the source and the Handler. Whilst accepting that in an investigation several interviews may take place with one witness, there does not exist, what could be referred to as a normal interpersonal relationship, between the Investigator and the interviewee. Sources are recruited to provide information and their relationship with a Handler can last anything from a few weeks to several years. During this period, each party comes to know the other. This existing relationship provides the essential *rapport* element that we will discuss later. However, it also has the potential to lead to such problems as complacency on the part of Handlers and the source, and the cross-contamination of what is obtained because of previous encounters.

Second, in the majority of investigations where a witness is interviewed, they will be providing information on a single event. For example, they have just observed a fatal road traffic collision. The nature of the questioning needs to focus exclusively on that single 'event'. As we highlighted in Chapter 4, when a Handler carries out the debriefing of a source there are likely to have been 'multiple events' that have occurred between meetings. Research by Connolly and Price (2006) has shown that it can be cognitively challenging to attribute details to a specific event where several similar events have occurred. In source debriefings, there is a greater likelihood of this problem occurring in situations where the source is reporting on many similar events, as opposed to when they are reporting on different events, events that occurred under different circumstances, or with different actors. Furthermore, problems are likely to be exacerbated the greater time difference that is left between the events occurring and the debriefing of the source, as this leads to memories degrading and merging.

Third, is the fact that in the investigative interview the information to be obtained will be because the person has witnessed the events and therefore has first-hand knowledge of those events. In the source debriefing, the source may have obtained the information they are imparting in many different ways. Some of it may be through direct observation, some of it may be because they actually participated in the events and some may be because they have overheard a conversation. With each of these, there will be memories that can be retrieved in similar ways to those used in an investigative interview. However, the source may also be passing information that they have heard from a third party i.e. 'hearsay'. Such information may or may not be of evidential worth, but it is still worthy of collection for intelligence purposes. Also, some of that which the source imparts may be speculation on their part because of their knowledge of those involved. This will be drawn from their semantic memory.

The fourth factor where investigative interviews and source debriefings are likely to vary, concerns the circumstances under which they take place. For the most part, an investigative interview will take place under controlled circumstances. It will be 'safe' from a physical attack occurring on those taking part. Concerns about who sees the interview process will be minimal or easily controlled. Moreover, the location will be relatively comfortable with chairs, tables, and adequate heat and light. More often than not, there will be a reasonable amount of time in which to carry out the interview in a constructive and organized manner. Furthermore, the interviewing officer will have had adequate time to plan the interview. This has to be contrasted with the nature of a source debriefing which is often carried out in uncomfortable and stressful situations, where there exists a real threat of physical harm to all present. The debriefing is likely to be time-limited, a problem compounded in some cases, by the Handler having little time to prepare for it beforehand. Time factors are likely to impact on the quality of information obtained (Kebell, Milne, and Wagstaff, 1997).

194

The fifth factor that needs to be considered is the likelihood that the source may well have taken part in the criminality which they are discussing. The majority of witnesses to a crime are not in any way, suspected of involvement in any criminality surrounding the event, which they are describing. The majority of sources are likely to be offenders of one type or another, and many are involved in serious crime. Whilst they may, or may not, have taken part in the actual event they are reporting on, they are likely to have taken part in similar events, with the potential for the contamination of one event with the other. Moreover, there can be a fine line between when a source passively observes criminality that is occurring and moves to a position where they may be legally culpable. Akin to suspects, this means that sources will be, by nature, cautious of what they are saying and guarded in some aspects of their reporting. They will instinctively resort to the 'less is better' rule. The less they tell the Handler the safer it is for them. Besides, there may well be legal ramifications if they admit their involvement in a crime. This creates a situation where they will distort some aspects of the reporting. While there is always a danger of a witness distorting events, this is much more is likely to occur in the source context. The need for self-protection will override a desire to provide full information. In some cases, this will be an ongoing issue.

Sixth, concerns prioritization. As has already been discussed with both an interview and a debrief, the time to conduct them may be limited. However, in the investigative interview, prior knowledge of the investigation will allow the interviewing officer to prioritize what information has to be gained. This can often be done before the interview commences. Where there is limited time in a source debrief, the source will often have to impart many events before the Handler can objectively decide on which event to concentrate. In doing so they will of necessity disrupt the *free recall* of the source. As we will discuss allowing free recall is an essential technique in maximizing memory recall. Compromises will have to be made. As a general rule, the Handler should always let the source begin the debrief where the source wants to begin, as that is what is most important to them.

The seventh distinction that can occur is, that many of the events on which the source is reporting, are not yet concluded. There is a real expectation that the source will gain more related information in the future. Handlers must take cognizance of the fact that the source will have to re-engage with these persons soon. The Handler must be careful not to give the source any information that the source does not know already. For example, the source may talk about a person called 'Felix' being present at a meeting, to which the Handler replies: 'He is from New York. Isn't he?' The source did not know this and if they let it slip later, it may place them in jeopardy. There is also the potential that because the source has recanted in detail the preceding events and discussed them at length, their thought processes will be unconsciously influenced by the Handler and this will affect their future behavior.

Finally, Handlers have to maintain the relationship. We want the source to be there tomorrow. The need for getting the maximum amount of truthful information must be balanced against the need to maintain the relationship. Pushing for more may create conflict. Accusing the source of deceit almost certainly will.

Undoubtedly all these factors add complexity to the task of debriefing and another reason why handling is not a job every officer can do. Even experienced interviewers will struggle to remember everything they have to do and the things they should not do.

Identifying effective techniques

The method of debriefing a source given here is based upon real-world research. It includes the use of several different techniques. Each technique was identified, labeled, and assessed against several criteria. Firstly, *'the theoretical soundness of the technique'*. Any technique suggested has a sound theoretical basis and there is evidence supporting its effectiveness. The mere fact that a technique is widely used in law enforcement will not necessarily fulfill this criterion. The second criterion is *'the utility of the technique'*. Each technique must be capable of being used in the vast majority of source debriefing contexts. To explain this; the following example may be useful. A technique that is often used in the investigative interview of children is to have purpose-built and decorated rooms conducive to warmth and safety. This technique works in the interview of a child but is impractical in the source debriefing context; it fails to meet the utility criterion. If a technique has utility experienced Handlers should be able to recognize almost immediately how they could use the technique, and the benefits that would accrue from it. The third criterion is *'ease of transfer'*. Can the technique be readily taught to officers engaged in source debriefing? We must be able to demonstrate that the time spent training the technique provides a suitable return on the investment. Given the amount Handlers already need to learn, there will always be competition as to what to include in training and what to leave out. Fourth, there must be the *'capacity to integrate'* the technique with the other techniques used in managing sources. There is little point in shoehorning in a technique, to the detriment of other techniques. The debrief needs to work as seamlessly as possible.

The overarching goal of using any identified technique is that it assists in obtaining the maximum amount of accurate information, while at the same time contributing to the effective management of that source.

The cognitive interview

In Chapter 4 we discussed how memories were encoded before being stored. If we want to access these memories, we must find a way to them. Metaphorically, what we have is lots of locked boxes with different pathways to them. The code for these boxes is stored at the same time the memory is created.

If we want the content to a particular memory, we must first find the pathway to the memory box, and then enter the code that unlocks the box. A source will have encoded and stored many events. Handlers must then guide the source through the retrieval of the memories associated with each of those events. One tried and tested method that has proved successful in many law enforcement investigative contexts is the *cognitive interview*. The core principle of the cognitive interview is the 'guided retrieval' of memories.

The cognitive interview was originally developed by Fisher, Geiselman, and their associates (1984). They list four key elements that aid memory retrieval: *context reinstatement, reporting everything, recalling the incident from different perspectives,* and *changing the temporal order of recall.* The cognitive interview has been modified in several ways over the years to address problems with it, and the application of it (Fisher and Geiselman, 1992). The primary changes have included the need for the inclusion of interpersonal/communication-based psychology, in its application.

Research has established the effectiveness of the cognitive interview in the interviews of witnesses, victims, and suspects. Cognitive interviewing reliably enhances the process of memory retrieval and elicits more information without generating inaccurate accounts. It works. However, as we have already pointed out, source debriefing is different from these other types of interviews. What is needed is an adaptation of the cognitive interview to address the

199

specific problems encountered in source debriefing. Most notably are the number of events that the source reports on, the progressive nature of these events, and the ongoing need to maintain and develop the relationship with the source. As we create methods to address these issues, we will explore in greater depth how to contemporaneously apply the key elements of the cognitive interview.

Before we progress, it must be stressed that what is suggested here is intended to be practical. Handlers should aim to use these methods as a standard way of carrying out a debrief. In the beginning, it may feel clunky for both Handlers and source, but over time it becomes second nature for the Handlers and many sources come to accept it, and the quality and quantity of their reporting increases accordingly. However, life with sources is not always straight forward. What is proposed here has in-built flexibility. For example, if time is short the Handler needs to put maximum focus on what has the highest priority. If there is a major welfare problem for the source, use the time to focus on that. If there is an urgent need for information on a certain gang, focus on that. Flexibility is key to the application of the suggested methodology.

Cognitive Debriefing Model

A model is a representation of a concept, created to aid the understanding of it. It is a simplified description of more complex ideas. When it comes to explaining how a Handler should debrief a source, we will have recognized by now that there is a lot is going on, and a lot to remember especially when in an operational environment. It can be difficult to take it all in. The model is designed to help us remember what we have to do. However, by their nature models omit detail. The model we will use attempts to take in as many of the factors at play as possible. It is intended to guide us through the debrief of a source.

This model has five stages and there are 22 steps in it. This is an indication of the complexity of the task that is being undertaken. Debriefing a source is not about having a chat. It involves a combination of complex psychology, interpersonal skills, and fieldcraft. In naming the model we have considered several factors. First the 'cognitive' element of what we are trying to achieve; the word cognitive meaning connected with thinking or conscious mental processes. Second, many of the elements used are drawn from the cognitive interview. Third, there are distinct differences between interviewing and debriefing. The name makes it clear, it is not interviewing. The model is called the 'Cognitive Debriefing Model'

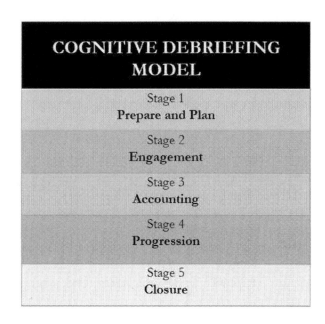

Figure 5.3 The 5 Stage Cognitive Debriefing Model

Stage one involves the preparation and planning before the debrief. Stage two, engagement, involves the initial contact with the source at the meeting location. Stage three is when we access the information that the source has stored in their memory, using techniques drawn from cognitive interviewing. Stage four is about discussing with the source how to progress with what has been learned and what further tasks the source should undertake. Stage five is about ending the debriefing on a positive note. It is about strengthening the relationship and ensuring the safety of all involved, as they go their separate ways.

In using this model, we will refer to the source recalling 'events'. We can think of an event in a similar way that we would consider an episode of our favorite television series. Events may take place over a prolonged period or come in rapid succession. A source may have met their associates the previous week, and then again, the previous evening. This would be considered as two events. However, in the case where a source meets first with two associates and they then drive to a bar where a third associate joins them, these may also be considered as two events.

Handlers must enter the debriefing process in a friendly non-combative way. It is not an interrogation. It is not about forcing the source to give up information. If it is, the Handlers have failed to properly recognize and address the source's motives for giving information. The priority should be to first address this problem and only then seek information. If the source's motives are not being addressed there is every chance they will lie, misdirect, and deceive the Handler, in whatever way they can. Time is then wasted trying to sort the wheat from the chaff, only to find that the wheat that is there, is full of weevils.

Stage 1 Prepare and Plan

As the name implies Stage One is about ***preparing and planning*** for the debrief. All of stage one is done before the meeting. There are 4 steps.

STAGE 1 PREPARE & PLAN	
Step 1	Relationship Management
Step 2	Intelligence Requirement
Step 3	Equipment
Step 4	Operational Plan

Figure 5.4 Stage 1 Prepare and Plan

Step 1 is about *relationship management*. The Handlers and the Controller discuss the current state of the source relationship, both from a welfare perspective and a productivity perspective. There may be concerns around the current behavior of the source, or there may be unresolved matters from previous meetings. Previous contact notes should be looked at to identify any issues. The Handlers and Controller should discuss the various options to deal with these matters and decide on a course of action. The purpose of the meeting should be identified, and what is expected to be gained from it agreed.

Step 2 is about identifying what information the agency expects to get as a result of the meeting. There may be specific questions that the Intelligence Unit wants to be answered. These *intelligence requirements* should come in writing and be prioritized. Besides, there may be other operational tasks that the Controller wants the source to undertake. For example, they may want the source to visit a particular bar and obtain the layout of it. Included in discussions around the intelligence requirements will always be the question of feasibility. Is the source capable of carrying out the task safely?

Step 3 is about identifying any ***equipment*** the Handlers need to take with them. This will include any money to cover expenditure, or to give to the source. It may also include photos or maps to show to the source. The Handler should also have a pen and paper, as this may be needed should the source want to draw something out. If the debrief is to be audio or video recorded, the equipment should be tested beforehand. If handwritten notes are to be used, the preferred option is a secure electronic notebook. Handlers will also need the mobile phone they use to contact the source. They may also need radios to liaise with any defensive surveillance officers they have in place to protect the meeting.

Step 4 is the creation of an ***operational plan*** for the debriefing. This includes a discussion of how the source will come into physical contact with the Handlers, and where and how the debriefing will take place. It will also involve discussions around what defensive surveillance is needed to protect all those taking part. When everything has been agreed instructions are given to the source regarding the time and the place. Their agreement is obtained, and the Handler confirms the source understands everything clearly. It is easy to get the details mixed up, which can add a lot of stress to the meeting before it even starts.

This also helps reassure the source of the Handler's professionalism.

Stage 2 Engagement

The cognitive interview stresses the need to build rapport with the subject, and to explain to them what will occur during the interview. Stage Two, the *engagement* stage, mirrors much of that. It has the goal of creating a context conducive to obtaining information. However, equally important at each meeting with a source is the maintenance of the existing relationship and the potential further development of it. It requires substantial effort on the part of a Handler to ensure that a source remains committed to the relationship. In addressing the source's needs first, this has the added benefit of assuring the source that their needs matter, and this in turn helps ensure their commitment to the debrief process. It is much easier for the Handler to create reasons for the source to pass good information than to have to drag the source kicking and screaming to give up every detail. It is always better to give first.

Before progressing further into Stage 2 it is an apt time to mention a skill that is fundamental to source management: *active listening.*[13] Handlers need to know how to listen. Few do. Police officers are

---

[13] A full chapter in the book the Human Source Management System (Buckley 2006) is devoted to this topic. This should convey how important it is in managing sources.

notoriously bad at listening. They listen for what they think they need, with little regard to what the other person is trying to convey. Unfortunately, listening is not something that many of us do consistently well. Listening is not about hearing; it is something much more taxing on the brain. People who say they are good listeners, usually aren't. They miss key points. Listening is not about us. It's not about congratulating ourselves on how well we have done something. Active listening is a process that can assist us in gaining a much better understanding of what a person is trying to convey. If we do it well, we also have the potential to pick up on what a person is trying to keep hidden.

Here are a few of the key elements to listen more effectively. Take time. Listening to someone takes time; if we are in a rush, we won't be listening. Avoid distractions. If a lot is going on around us, or we have a lot of competing issues in our head, we won't be able to listen. Be present in the moment. The Handler has only one job to do: 'I am here to listen to this person. Nothing else is as important at this time.' Listen to the words used. If we can't repeat verbatim, the last four words that the person has said, we have not listened.

Listen to the voice tone and speed of speech. Approximately 40% of what we are saying comes from the way we say something. If there is a change in intonation, there is also a change in meaning. Observe non-verbal communication. Approximately 50% of communication is conveyed non-verbally, through facial and body movements, and the accompanying gestures. If we miss these, we miss the meaning. Listen to hear what is said, not to formulate a reply. We all tend to listen to half of what the person is saying, then start formulating how we will respond. If we listen to a person, they will tell us what they need or want. But if we listen superficially, we will get the wrong answer.

A Handler needs to listen extremely well, not only to address to know the source's needs and fears but to hear where potential details have been omitted concerning the information the source is providing. If the Handler listens consistently throughout the debrief it is much easier to pick up inconsistencies in what the source is saying, and indicators of potential deception.

Listening is mentally exhausting. If the Handler has been listening properly, they will feel mentally drained after a debrief. It follows that if the Handler is already tired before the meeting, or they are distracted by other matters, then they are less likely to perform well during the debrief. We return now to Stage Two.

STAGE 2 ENGAGEMENT	
Step 5	Entrance
Step 6	Security
Step 7	Relationship & Welfare
Step 8	Agenda
Step 9	Explanation

Figure 5.5 Stage 2 Engagement

Step 5, the *entrance,* is the initial physical contact between source and Handler. For the meeting to take place both parties have to meet. On occasions, this may be a quite simple process. For example, the source may be walking along a road where the Handlers pick him up in a car. This is what we refer to as the entrance and it includes what is said to the source including, taking care to use effective non-verbal communication. It will involve a greeting, and perhaps a handshake or similar gesture. This coming together of Handlers and source can carry with it, substantial risk. More often than not, operational methodology, of which the source may not be aware, will be used. The way the entrance is conducted will impact on the debriefing. If all goes to plan, the source will be relaxed. If it goes to hell in a handcart most of the already limited debriefing time will be spent calming the source. The Handlers too will feel the effect. If a Handler is not apprehensive about the entrance, they are complacent about safety.

Simple things make an entrance work more smoothly. If the Handlers have discussed beforehand who will do what, and say what, it is much more likely to run smoothly. Thinking about the proxemics involved in the meeting are important. Proxemics are the effects that space/proximity have on behavior, communication, and social interaction. Handlers need to think about who will sit where, and the impact that will have. Also, Handlers want to create an ambiance that is conducive to a positive meeting. For example, the provision of refreshments. Breaking bread with someone is basic human behavior and a sign of trust and friendship.

Step 6 relates to the *security* of the meeting. Security is the primary concern in any source debriefing and is the first element to be addressed when contact is commenced with the source. Handlers need to check if the source has any immediate security concerns, and if there are, these need to be addressed forthwith. If the source does not feel safe, they will be preoccupied with regaining their safety. This is obviously detrimental to the debriefing process. At this time Handlers need to check with the source how much time the source can safely spend 'off-grid' and that they have a valid reason if anyone asks them, as to where they have been. As a minimum, the source should also check that their phone is locked. Pocket dials have compromised many different relationships.

Step 7 is about the *relationship* with the source and their *welfare.* This is when the Handlers focus on building rapport with the source. This should be source centric. It is about their needs and concerns. If the source has ongoing issues of one sort or another, the Handlers should attempt to rectify them as best as possible. This frees up the source's mind to concentrate on the forthcoming task.

This is an important step because it allows the Handlers to judge the mood of the source. Most of us change our mood from day-to-day. Some days we are on the top of the world and nothing can knock us back; on other days we feel like drowning ourselves in a bottle of gin, with Leonard Cohen music for background noise. Sources are no different. Some days up, some days down. Sometimes the Handler is their best friend and on others, they would quite happily see the Handler dead, literally. When a Handler spends enough time with a source, they get to know the source's 'normal'. Knowing the baseline allows the Handler to detect variations from that baseline. The Handlers should use this time building rapport and identifying the mood of the source.

Step 8 the *agenda,* is where the Handler sets out the order of business for the debriefing. It will normally begin with the reason for the meeting, if it is not obvious. The time available for the debriefing will vary from meeting to meeting, and the Handler will have priorities about what information must, should, and could, be obtained. The Handler should explain to the source the intended course of the debrief including the different things they want to talk about. In most cases, this will relax the source. If there is an issue that may cause stress to the source, there is no point in introducing it and then saying: 'We will talk about that later.' The source will be focussed solely on it. The Handler needs to deal with it then and there, before progressing, or not mention it until they are in a position to talk about it fully.

Step 9 is the *explanation* step. The Handler tells the source how Stage 3 of the process will be carried out. In the beginning, the Handler will have to give more detailed explanations. The source may feel awkward about what they are being asked to do or feel that it is silly. As with all aspects of source management, it is for the Handler to find the balance regarding what the likely level of source understanding will be and where the relationship is. It stands to reason we do not want to overwhelm a source in the early stages of the relationship. While technical language is used here to explain ideas, the Handler will have to find appropriate ways of explaining the concepts to the source. Giving the source an easily understood explanation of what is happening, makes it more likely that they will engage with the process. The source should be given an opportunity to ask questions or to clarify what they have to do. If the source is asking questions about the process it is a strong indicator that they are engaging with it. As a source relationship grows and as the source becomes familiar with the methodology involved, the time taken for this phase will be significantly reduced.

The Handler should explain what we mean by the technique of *reporting everything*. This is a critical part of cognitive interviewing. Often the source may only wish to give details of which they are absolutely certain. They will not give incomplete details. The Handler should explain to the source that some people hold back on information because they don't know what is important or what may be useful. The source should be encouraged to provide even trivial details that lie within their knowledge. The information the source provides is contributing to a jigsaw, and any small piece they provide may be the piece the Intelligence Unit has been waiting for. The Handler should tell the source to assume that they, the Handler, does not know anything. The source is likely to feel encouraged if the Handler uses phrases such as: 'I wasn't there. I don't know what happened. You were. Tell me everything.'

At the outset it can be beneficial for the Handler to provide an example of what they mean by the term report everything. For example if they are in a café, the Handler may identify to the source a customer sitting at the far side of the restaurant with a friend. Rather than saying, 'There are two men at the table talking to each other they are both about 30 years old and they have been talking for five minutes.' They should begin the example thus:

'There are two people at the table. The table is square, it is against the wall, and there are three upright chairs. There is a lamp directly over the table. It is about 3 meteres from the door. Two men are sitting directly opposite each other. The man facing the door is approximately 30 years old. He has receding, brown hair, cut short. He is clean shaven. His features are Hispanic. He is wearing a brown jacket, blue collared short, jeans and brown shoes. He is right-handed...'

The Handler continues illustrating the depth of description that is expected. Using this technique shows the source what is expected and encourages them to provide greater recall.

It should also be explained to the source, not to be concerned about having the vocabulary to express ideas. They should be encouraged to illustrate and complement what they are saying, using non-verbal communication.

Ideally, the source would have unlimited time but rarely this is the case. Nevertheless, they should be encouraged not to rush and to report everything they think of. Often a source will leave out detail that they assume the Handler already knows, or would not be interested in. The instruction from the Handler to report everything, no matter how trivial it seems, enhances the chances of maximizing information. With sources who have been met many times they soon become conditioned to reporting everything and a one or two-word reminder is then all that is needed.

A word of warning is required. While *report everything* is an essential element of cognitive interviewing methodology, the source may admit their involvement in a crime. Setting aside the ethical issues in this, having to deal with an admission adds complexity to the situation. We do not want the source to break their flow but admitting their involvement in an offense will well cause problems. It is worth discussing this with the source before it happens.

From a debriefing perspective, there are some add on benefits to the report everything method. There are occasions when a Handler knows of exiting intelligence, which they want to add to. However, they are unable to ask the source directly about it because to open discussion on that topic, may jeopardize the other source of information and as a minimum, it educates the source as to its existence. Also, many sources live complex lives. They can have access to information on which the Handler has no awareness. They assume that because the Handler has not asked about it, they are not interested. By encouraging the source to report everything, new information-gathering opportunities potentially open up.

Finally, the source should be told that it is ok if they cannot remember something. If sources feel pressurized to give complete information, it will be damaging to their esteem, if they can't remember some detail They will be tempted to omit the bit they do know, failing to mention anything on the topic, or they will add to the limited information they have so that it appears complete. They will make it up.

Stage 3 Accounting

Stage 3 *accounting* focuses on obtaining the information. How long this stage takes will be dependent on the length of time since the last meeting, the number of times there has been telephone contact, and how busy the source has been. It can be difficult to know where to start as there could be things the source wants to tell, and they may not be the same as the things the Handler wants to know. It may seem easier to have everything told in chronological order, but it is best to let the source start where they want to start. They know what they want to tell and the least that is done to disrupt their recall the better. In addition, culture may play a part in where the source sees the event beginning. Something that happened some time ago, may have relevance in how they perceive the story. Let the source start and then progress from there, examining each event in turn.

While the Handler is listening, they should act out what is happening in their brain, creating pictures of what was occurring. This will include imagining the people that were present and the place where they were. This makes the tale more interesting and it will be easier to spot gaps and anomalies in the narrative.

STAGE 3 ACCOUNTING	
Step 10	Context Reinstatement
Step 11	Free Recall
Step 12	Questioning
Step 13	Varied Retrieval & Clarification
Step 14	Confirmation and Comment

Figure 5.6 Stage 3 Accounting

Step 10 is the *context reinstatement.* This is another critical part of the cognitive interview. The theory asserts that the closer the context is in which the memory is recalled, to when the memory was encoded, then the greater the quality of the recall is likely to be. People are usually able to remember more information if they are in the same place as when they learned it or first created the memory. The concept here is that what the source was experiencing at the time of the event is likely to provide links to when the memory was stored. If the storage context can be recreated, then the links to the memories can be created and the memories accessed. The positive effects of context reinstatement would suggest that if we debriefed sources where the event occurred and under similar circumstances, more information would be obtained. However, this is practically impossible. To overcome this the Handler should ask the source to *mentally* reinstate the context of the event. We want the source to picture the place where the event occurred, as clearly as possible in their mind. If the source is encouraged to envision everything that was happening at the time of the event, the more of the event they are likely to remember. This mental reinstatement could include how the source was feeling on the day of the event, what they were wearing, what sounds there were, and what the weather was like.

The Handler will say to the source something akin to: 'I want you to think back to before you met Hassan. Put yourself back there. Think about everything that was going on. Everything you were hearing and seeing. Think about how you were feeling and what you were wearing. If it makes it easier close your eyes. In your mind recreate the circumstances.' The only downside of context reinstatement is the time it takes. The Handler must decide if they have sufficient time to use it, concerning each event.

The final element of this step is to hand control over to the source. The source must know that they are free to talk for as long as it is needed, and that they have control over the way they tell what they have to tell. If they feel constrained in any way, that will constrain their delivery of the information.

Step 11 is *free recall.* Free recall occurs when the source is allowed to recount information without interruption. The fewer controlling cues the Handler gives, the purer subsequent product will be. Free recall is a fundamental technique of the cognitive interview but if it is to be used successfully Handlers have to be trained not to interrupt or to interject, in a conversation. Some officers find this all but impossible. They have an almost obsessive need to control every aspect of an interaction. Officers in this phase must use active listening techniques including non-verbal encouragement. Any inappropriate interruptions break the source's concentration and reinforce the undesirable perception of Handler domination. If this is done properly, and as the relationship progresses, the source will 'learn' that they can give a full account, without interruption, or concerns about who is dominant.

During free recall the source should be encouraged to start from where they want, and the Handler should let them splurge. At this time, no effort should be made to try and separate events. As has already been discussed, if the Handler interrupts it is almost impossible for the source to retrieve the same information.

Step 12 is about *questioning* the source to obtain greater detail about what has happened. This should be done in a non-confrontational way, continuing to encourage the source to report everything. Questions should be used subtlety. They are not meant to be a blunt instrument. If poor questions are asked, they will

218

distort the way a memory is recalled. How the Handler asks a question can convey judgment, which will discourage the source from responding in an open way. Poorly structured questions will confuse the source and if it happens regularly, it will damage the source's trust in the Handler.

Given the fact that questioning is an essential part of law enforcement, it is perhaps surprising how bad most officers are at it. While there is insufficient space here to explore the issue in-depth, there are some types of questions that should, as a general rule, be avoided. Closed questions require one-word answers, normally a yes or a no. Leading questions are questions that suggest an answer. 'Did Joe put the drugs in the car?' Here the source is consciously or unconsciously triggered to confirm that Joe put the drugs into the car. In reality, Joe may have been present but *he did not* put the drugs into the car.

The more *open* a question the Handler asks the more likely it is that the source's answer will be more accurate and more complete. Open questions will take the source a longer period to recall, and there will be latency between when the question is asked and answered as the source searches their memory for the detail. Open questions include the use of words such as 'tell', 'explain' and 'describe'. 'Tell me about, Patrick.' 'Explain exactly what happened in the bar.' 'Describe Chico's brother.'

Appropriate open questions should be used to encourage further recall, before funneling down into each aspect through more specific questioning. For example, the Handler may begin by asking the source: 'How did Serge get to the bar?' This question leaves the source free to reply without being led in any direction. When the source answers: 'He drove there.', the Handler can follow through with a question such as: 'What type of vehicle did he use?' Each time the Handler has to be careful not to implant information into the source's memory and thus distort what is there. An inappropriate question would be 'Did Serge drive to the bar?' as this may lead to a distortion in the source's memory.

During this step, the Handler should ascertain the *provenance* of the information, if it has not been made already apparent. The Handler should clarify with the source how they obtained the information. The discussion about provenance should include the circumstances under which the information was obtained, as these may have influenced the source's perception of the event. It should be remembered that while the source is retelling one story, they may have obtained bits of that story, at different times, in different ways, and are now conflating it into one seemingly complete narrative.

The Handler should ask all questions relevant to one event at one time. If they jump from event to event, this will break the momentum of the source and impede accurate recall. The Handler should avoid brushing over things that they think they already know. The source may have additional information or conflicting information. Also, it may alert the source, to the existence of another source.

Step 13 is entitled *varied retrieval and clarification*. There are two elements in this step. Varied retrieval involves using techniques to access a memory differently, while clarification seeks to eliminate any ambiguities. There are three techniques used in varied retrieval. If time permits all three can be used or the Handler may choose which technique to use depending on what they are seeking to achieve. The first varied retrieval technique is referred to as *change perspective.* Change perspective involves getting the source to retell the information from a different perspective. This changed perspective can cue the recall of additional details. It causes the source to access different aspects of memory and uses different cues. For example, the source is asked to imagine seeing the event from another's perspective. 'Tell me what the waiter would have seen.' Alternatively, they are asked to imagine what they would have seen had they been viewing it from a different place. 'Imagine you had been across the room, what would you have seen?'

The second technique is referred to as *change temporal order.* We all tend to work from the beginning of an event through to the end. By asking the source to tell the story from the end and backward, they may recall different details. Alternatively, we can ask them to start from the point that is most salient for them. This is actually where many people will start a story normally.

The third technique is the use of *retrieval prompts*. Retrieval prompts involve using cues to stimulate how the source accesses memory Asking a source to act out what happened may aid recall. 'Act out what happened from when you came into the room.' The source gets up and goes to the door and acts out the event from there. ' I came in. Joe was on my right and Pedro was on the left. Mike was up at the bar...' Another useful retrieval prompt is to get the source to draw out the location. The source is told to include anything they want and describe everything as they are drawing it. They then talk through what happened using the sketch as an aid. As they do so they generate their retrieval cues.

Asking the source to think in terms of the 5 senses i.e. hearing, seeing, smell, taste, and touch will help in their recollection of the event. Such thoughts are all intended to stimulate the source's thinking in different ways and thus retrieving additional memory. For example, asking a source to think about smell may jar a memory concerning the smell of a particular chemical being used in counterfeiting. Other methods that the Handler can use to draw out more detail. include, concerning a person's description - asking who a person looked similar too, about remembering a name - imagining how that name sounded and/or how many syllables were in it, These easy to grasp techniques are likely to be of practical use to any Handler in a debrief and will increase the amount of information recalled.

Accessing Detail	
People	**Conversation**
Physical appearance.	Who was present and for how long?
Remind you of anyone.	Seating.
Clothing.	What was said and by whom.
Behavior.	Notable speech characteristics.
Anything unusual.	Language used or accent.
Anything carried.	Particular words or phrases used.
	Names or numbers referred to.
	Reactions.
	Conflicts.
	Side-taking.
Thoughts	**Senses**
What was source thinking at time?	Images.
What were they feeling?	Sounds.
Why?	Smells.
What might others have been thinking?	Tastes.
	Skin sensations.

Table 5.1 Accessing detail

The Handler then seeks to clarify any anomalies in the account. Care needs to be taken as this may sound to the source as if they are being challenged. It is useful for the Handler to have a few stock phrases they can use that are likely to take the potential sting out of any clarifying remark. 'I just want to take you back to what you said about Maria. Can you go over that again?' 'I think I am a bit confused can you …' 'I think I missed a bit…' What the Handler is doing is taking ownership of the lack of clarity. This is likely to seem less threatening to the source. In reality, the Handler has identified ambiguity that needs clarification. Echoing the source's words is another way of seeking clarification. 'You said that Jacob was 'fucking furious'…' The source will further explain the meaning they intended from the words. Care needs to be taken in seeking clarification because if too much time is spent on a specific point, the source will know how important that point is to the Handler. At this point, the second Handler may want to interject with something they have spotted that has been missed.

Step 14 is about ***confirmation and comment***. When the source has finished recalling *each* event the Handler must seek confirmation that they have recorded the facts correctly. On commencing this step, the Handler should tell the source to interrupt them if they remember any new information, or there are any errors in the information that the Handler is recanting. If the source interrupts, the Handler should stop talking and listen. The source needs to feel they can speak freely, and we do not want them to forget whatever thought has crept into their head. It may be impossible to retrieve it later.

The Handler should systematically go through each event, summarising the details as they go. Where it is appropriate, the Handler may add commentary. This is a way of drawing out any further thoughts that the source may have on the matter and of checking that the Handler has understood both the facts and the feelings involved. The source should be invited to add their opinion to the information. A source 'comment' forms an integral part of any source debriefing. In many cases, the source will have expert or additional knowledge, of the event or the people involved. This additional knowledge allows the source to provide an educated comment on the facts that they have related. Whilst this comment may have no relevance from an evidential perspective, it can be extremely useful from an intelligence perspective.

A significant difference in Stage 3, from the other stages, is its potential for repetition. Each of the other stages is progressive. The repetition of this stage is essential to address multiple events that the source may have information on. The stage is designed in such a way as to enable the Handler to finish obtaining information on one event, then return to address what has occurred in the next event, etc. Each time, the extent to which the techniques are used will vary depending upon the complexity of the event and operational constraints. In short, the Handler has different tools for different jobs.

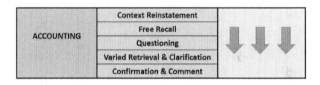

ACCOUNTING	Context Reinstatement	
	Free Recall	
	Questioning	
	Varied Retrieval & Clarification	
	Confirmation & Comment	

Figure 5.7 Stage 3 Repeated

Once the source has completed their recall of all events and if they have not answered any of the intelligence requirements identified in Step 2, this is the time to address them. This is also the time to ask about any previous tasks given to the source if they have not been mentioned. The Handler should choose the interviewing techniques that are most appropriate to ascertain this information. Examples of a topic addressed may include: 'Have you heard anything about the robbery at the jewelry shop, last week?' asked

225

to a source whose main area of reporting is drug importation. Similarly, 'Have you heard anything about the murder of that prostitute?' asked to a source whose main area of reporting is burglary. In both cases, there is potential for the source to have heard pieces of information, but because it is outside their normal area of reporting, they may assume the information will be of no interest to the Handler. When all the information has been acquired, the Handler then moves to Stage 4.

Stage 4 Progression

Stage 4 *progression* recognizes the fact that there is an ongoing relationship with the source. Further tasks have to be completed and more information obtained, by the source. The Handler and source are now in a position to discuss what more can be done to obtain more information.

STAGE 4 PROGRESSION	
Step 15	Consultation
Step 16	Tasking
Step 17	Training
Step 18	Recognition and Reward

Figure 5.8 Stage 4 Progression

Step 15 *consultation* relates to discussions between the Handler and source as to what the source could and should do next. In this step, the Handler will be aware of possible opportunities to gather more information. Discussion with the source involves both parties coming up with ideas as to what potentially, may be the best course of action. The Handler will want to maximize the information while the source will have concerns about their safety, and other things that may impact on their ability to complete any task. For example, family commitments. The Handler must listen to what the source has to say. The source will have a good understanding of what they can or cannot achieve. If the Handler knows the source well, then there should be little cause for dispute. Sources know things that are likely to bring them under adverse notice or that will raise suspicion with their criminal associates.

Step 16 *tasking* involves giving the source details of the specific tasks that the Handler wants the source to carry out in an agreed period. Tasking is fundamental to a productive source relationship. Any task given to the source must be realistic and lie within the capabilities of the source. The source must agree to the task. If the source does not agree to undertake it, there is little point in giving it to them. They will only find some way out of it. Where a specific task may place the source in additional danger, prior approval should be obtained from the Controller. The Handler should be clear about what tasks have the highest priority.

Step 17 *training* involves equipping the source with the skills necessary to perform the role of a source safely and efficiently. Sources need continual training in operational aspects of their role and for specific tasks. Also, some techniques can be taught to the source to improve their ability to memorize events. A record of any training given to a source should be included in the contact note for that meeting.

Step 18 *recognition and reward* is where the Handler recognizes the value of the information given by the source and the effort made in obtaining it. Recognition is essential to address the motives of the source concerning 'self-esteem' and a feeling of 'belonging' to a team. It is at this point that the source may be given a monetary reward or discussion about future rewarding can take place. The timing of this is important from two perspectives. First, the source can see clearly what they are being rewarded for: 'You have just given information, and here is the reward.' (Obviously, not articulated in this way.) The source can make a direct link between cause and effect. This forms part of a regime that is intended to increase productivity. Second, the fact that the information acquisition process is complete means that the source cannot retrospectively withhold information because they are unsatisfied with the reward, nor can they embellish the information to get a greater reward. Where the source is to receive payment for expenses it should also be done at this time.

Stage 5 Closure

Stage 5 *closure* is a simple stage intended to draw proceedings to a close. It involves a gradual closing down of the debriefing and moving towards neutral topics and rapport building. At the end of this stage, all parties should feel relaxed and secure and they should know how things will progress in the future.

STAGE 5 CLOSURE	
Step 19	Rapport
Step 20	Future Contact
Step 21	Security
Step 22	Exit

Figure 5.9 Stage 5 Closure

Step 19 returns to the issue of *rapport*. The Handler should concentrate on personal and social issues relating to the source. If the meeting is solely about business, there is limited incentive for the source to deliver anything other than the bare minimum. Handlers need to get to know the source and the source needs to know that the Handler is genuine in concern for their wellbeing. This step is about lightening the mood and allowing all parties space to relax.

Step 20 relates to *future contact* with the source. The Handler and the source should agree as to when the source will next be in contact and offer tentative agreement as to when the next meeting will take place. Prolonged periods without contact will fail to strengthen the relationship and it will likely peter out. The source should be reminded that if something else comes to mind about what they have discussed during the debriefing, they should get in touch immediately.

Step 21 returns to the issue of the **security** of the source. The Handler's final comments should relate to the safety of the source. The Handler should check that the source has no pressing security concerns and that all fieldcraft measures have been taken account of.

Step 22 *exit* is the act of source and Handlers parting company. The source will normally leave the Handlers and if it is a public place the source will exit that location first. There should be no hesitations or awkwardness, or anything that would draw the eye of a third party. The source returns into their world. At this point, the debriefing is over. The Handlers must then return securely, to their place of work.

The model completed

What we have discussed here is a model designed for use in the debriefing of sources. It has taken good practice from other domains and combined investigative interviewing techniques with the operational realities of the source world. When we see it all together our initial impression may be that it is an extensive process. However, because Handlers are repeating the steps over and over again, they rapidly become adept at doing the right thing at the right time. Sources too, become habituated to the process and this removes the need to consider each step as a specific step. In an ongoing relationship, one step of this model will flow seamlessly into the next.

Prepare and Plan	Relationship Management	
	Intelligence Requirement	
	Equipment	
	Operational Plan	
Engagement	Entrance	
	Security	
	Relationship and Welfare	
	Agenda	
	Explanation	
Accounting	Context Reinstatement	
	Free Recall	
	Questioning	
	Varied Retrieval and Clarification	
	Confirmation and Comment	
Progression	Consultation	
	Tasking	
	Training	
	Recognition and Reward	
Closure	Rapport	
	Future Contact	
	Security	
	Exit	

Figure 5.10 Expanded Cognitive Debriefing Model

Having said all that some problems will remain. First, one of the main problems with the cognitive interviewing techniques that have been identified as being useful, is that they take time to carry out. Source meets are often rushed affairs. Handlers must find a balance between the time they have and how much information can be obtained at that time. Second, using this method, as with many of the other changes suggested in this book, will be hard for some to swallow. Officers sometimes find it difficult to accept that there may be a better way of doing something, and even if they acknowledge there is, putting in the additional effort may be a step too far. This reluctance to change will be exacerbated by the need for additional training for Handlers.

When it comes to using the cognitive interview techniques, we need to remember that there is potential for significant flexibility in its use. Where a situation dictates, we can use the bits we need and leave out the other bits. As Milne and Bull (2003) conclude it is perfectly acceptable to adopt the standpoint of asking which cognitive interview technique should be used, when they should be used and how they should be used. If we have the time and capturing all everything is required, we now have the tools to do it.

The role of the second Handler

Most of this process will be led by one Handler. The second Handler should play a full part in the rapport pieces but step back in obtaining the information. In some circumstances, their key function will be security. However, this does not mean that they do not listen to what is being said. Often the lead Handler will miss points that need clarification or miss a reaction from the source. When Handlers become used to working as a team, they develop an understanding of each other's behavior, knowing when to interject and how to interject, without breaking the flow. The second Handler may make note of salient points as the debrief progresses. If a recording device is not being used, then they will have to make a lot of notes. There will also be times when the lead Handler hits a mental block. It happens. The second Handler needs to be able to step in and resolve the matter, allowing the other Handler to regroup their thoughts.

Post debriefing

After a debrief, Handlers should meet with the Controller to discuss what happened. If there were problems these should be aired and dealt with. If there are lessons to be learned they should be shared with the rest of the team. The most pressing need will be to address any concern regarding the safety of the source or any other person. The Controller should discuss with the Handlers the status of the relationship and obtain a brief synopsis of the information. If there is an urgent need to share some piece of information with an Investigator or other party, this should be prioritized and submitted as soon as possible to the Intelligence Unit. The rest of the information should then be processed and submitted in the normal way.

Telephone debriefs

Save where contact is initiated by a source, the Controller should always be notified when the Handler is going to contact a source. If the source initiates the call, the Controller should be notified immediately thereafter.

Where a source passes information over the telephone, it should be submitted in the normal way, even if the Handler knows it is incomplete. When the full details are obtained a supplementary information submission can be created and cross-referenced to the original submission. Where the source supplies information during an ongoing operation this information may be shared verbally to those who need to know it. A note of what has occurred should be made in the contact note and a written information submission should follow as soon as it is practical afterword. The date and time it was passed and to whom it was passed should be included in a comment.

Deception

There are a lot of myths out there about deception but one thing is certain, when we are managing a source, there will be deception. The very nature of source management means that most sources will attempt to deceive us at some stage. The reasons for this are legion and include covering up their involvement in criminal activity, attempts to get more money from the Handler, attempts to get revenge on some person, and fear. Well trained Handlers will create circumstances where the reasons for deceit can be meaningfully reduced. In addition, with training Handlers will be able to much more accurately detect indicators of truth and indicators of deception.

Let us begin with deception in its simplest form – lying. There are two forms of lying: *active lying* and *passive lying*.

234

Active lying is the one we are all familiar with. It is the telling of a straight-up, bare-faced lie. 'That crow is white.' This type of deception is easy to detect and is rarely used. What is used is passive lying: 'I can't remember seeing a crow.' 'Maybe there was a crow... I saw a starling. It was doing a lot of chirping...' 'I think there might have been a crow. I will look the next time.' Passive lying is about ommissions, evasions, and distortions and is much more difficult to detect.

These types of deception are motivated by several different factors. A lot of the time it is a reaction to how the Handler or the agency is treating them. 'If you are going to treat me like shit, I am going to lie to you.' In treating people badly we motivate them to lie. The source may also fear that if they are truthful the Handler will become angry with them for something they have done, or there will be other negative consequences. They will also be motivated to lie to protect family members or close friends. They will downplay their involvement and divert the blame onto others. The source that is motivated solely by money will lie to be rewarded. If Handlers understand human motives and motivation picking up the reasons for deceit becomes a lot easier to identify and manage.

Two other forms of deceit are common namely *unintentional deception* and *confabulation*. Unintentional deceit occurs when a source misremembers something and then finds difficulty in correcting it either because they are certain they were right, or because they fear the consequences of correcting it. Confabulation occurs when the source fills in gaps in their memory with things that are not correct. This is often done to avoid looking foolish or to please the Handler.

Handlers often unconsciously assist in the deception. Fatigue sets in during the debrief and they just cannot face working their way through another conflict. A Handler may hear a lie but almost instantaneously file it in the 'too difficult to deal with tray'. The Handler may realize what the source has said is incorrect, because they are already aware of the correct version of events. Rather than ask the source to go over the point again, the Handler thinks to themselves they will fix it later. This fails to establish why the source is making the error. Is it erroneous or deceptive?

How we detect deception is sensitive and we really shouldn't make these things any more readily available than they already are. While we will not discuss how to do it, it is important to understand that once it is suspected, decisions have to be made whether to challenge it or not, and the ways to challenge it. We can also say that using a polygraph with a source has limited utility, and is likely to seriously damage the relationship. Anyone that suggests using one has not thought through the consequences. Generally speaking, if we suspect the source is being deceitful the best strategy is to gather the evidence of that deceit, and then as a team, create a plan to deal with it. This requires the Handler to keep their cool and avoid reacting. Remember, nothing for the Handler is ever personal.

The historic debrief

In an ideal world, we want to know everything the source can tell us. They may have been involved in criminality for many years before they begin to cooperate, and they have a lot of history which may even after many years still have utility. For example, a source may assume we know who committed a murder because 'Everyone knows who did that...' - the 'everyone' here, referring to everyone in the source's social circle, at the relevant time. The source assumes because they knew, that law enforcement would also have known. Currently, many officers are not interested in asking the source about their knowledge of the past because it does not help the officers make their cases, today.' Handlers in Dedicated Source Units understand intelligence and are working for the whole agency. They want to get as much from a source as they can get, and they know how to do it.

Carrying out a historic debrief with the source is one way of obtaining information of an historic nature. In essence, it is about getting the source to tell everything that they have had any knowledge of, from no matter how far in the past. There needs to be a few things in place to do this. First, the relationship between the Handlers and the source needs to be solid. The source must feel sufficiently comfortable with the Handlers to open up. Some topics may be very difficult for the source to talk about. Second, the Handlers need to be prepared for what they may be told. They must have both the professional skills and the interpersonal skills to react properly to what they are told. Sometimes a historic debrief can bring up stuff no one predicted. Third, time is needed. If a source has been involved in crime for many years, it is likely that one session will not cover it all. If this is likely to be the case and circumstances allow it, then taking the source away for a few days to a safe location may be the best option. Fourth, a suitable location needs to be available. Everyone needs to feel secure and everyone will want to be able to talk freely, make notes, move about, eat, and use the bathroom. The ability to have 'time-outs' during the session is also useful. Things may get stressed or awkward and any party may need to take a break. The source may want to go for a walk to clear their head. No matter how good the Handlers are, the source is still likely to feel under a lot of pressure.

One of the biggest dangers in historic debriefing is in how to manage the element of admissions. Many sources will have been involved in crime before becoming a source. The obligations on the Handler will vary according to the jurisdiction they are operating in. How a Handler should deal with such disclosures must be dealt with in basic training. Expecting a Handler to spontaneously deal with it is unrealistic. There are simply too many variables. The Handler will have to balance the legal requirements and the maintenance of the relationship.

An analyst can assist a lot in making sense of a historic debrief. If conditions allow it and if the Handlers have laid the ground, there is no reason why an analyst cannot be present during it. The big advantage of having the analyst present is their skill set in putting

238

structure around seeming isolated pieces of information and to create visual images of it. For example, as the source begins speaking of their life in a particular gang, the analyst can contemporaneously prepare a timeline highlighting key events. This can be used later by the Handler to take the source back to that event and discuss it in greater detail. As we know with the nature of memory the source is not going to provide this debrief in chronological order. Different events will be discussed as the memory is triggered in the source's head. These events make sense to the source because they are following the pathways in their brain. However, for others, it will appear the source is jumping from one topic to another in a seemingly random way. The analyst can also start to link people to particular events, and this too opens up options to pursue greater detail. In creating visuals, we will often spot gaps in the information or that there are identifiable patterns. Any Handler who thinks they can do this without the aid of an analyst is either exceptional, or overconfident, or both.

Conclusion

This chapter assumes that the source is motivated to provide information to the Handler. If the source is not providing information in the desired way, it is because the Handler either has not correctly identified the source's motives or is not satisfactorily addressing those motives. This is a serious problem. While the techniques suggested here will not address this problem, what they will do is an aid in detecting that there are issues.

If the methods suggested here are not the way that source debriefs are currently being carried out within an agency, then there are potentially one of four things occurring. First, the safety of the source and or the Handlers is endangered. Second, the relationship is not being managed properly. Third, the maximum amount of accurate information is not being obtained. Fourth, all three of these issues are present. Now that we have obtained the information from the source, let us now discuss how we write it up.

6. Writing It Up

*Looking for an entirely reliable informant is like looking
for a chaste mistress. If they were virtuous, they would be
little use to you in the first place. An informant merely
provides information; It is our job to verify that
information...*

Clockwork Angel - Cassandra Clare

Introduction

In this chapter, we are going to look at what happens
after the debrief. We will consider how the information
should be written up and what happens to it then.
While some may think this is a very simple process, we
will see that if the agency is to gain the maximum
benefit from what has been collected, then it requires
a bit more work on behalf of all those involved.

Controller duties (1)

Upon return from a debrief, the Controller should
meet with the Handlers. The first point should be to
check if there were any security concerns with the
meeting, the second to see if there are any security or
welfare issues with the source, including any adverse
behavior on the part of the source, that impacts on the
relationship and finally if there is any information that
needs urgent attention from an operational standpoint.
If there is nothing urgent the Handlers are left to write

up the information. If there are serious issues these should be escalated to the Authorizing Officer.

Controller duties (2)

When the Handlers have completed the contact note and information submission, the Controller should verify the content with them and discuss it. The Controller should check for the completeness of the information and accuracy. Where they identify that some information the source may have had is not included, those items should be listed to be obtained from the source during the next contact. Where necessary the Controller may add a comment at any of the points in the information submission. This means that for any piece of information there may be a Source comment, a Handler comment, and a Controller comment. Each of these is intended to assist the Intelligence Unit in preparing the final intelligence reports.

Where the Handler has prepared intelligence reports, the Controller should check them and endorse each one as agreed or instruct the Handler as to the changes to be made. These are *draft* intelligence reports. The Intelligence Unit should prepare the final ones. This ensures an independent assessment of the content.

There should be continuous contact between the Controller and the Intelligence Unit regarding any information submitted. Communication reduces the potential for misunderstandings

242

Content principles

There are a few principles the Handler should be aware of when it comes to writing up contact notes and information submissions. ***Completeness*** is important. The Handler was present at the meeting, the reader was not. The reader should be able to read the content, without the need for further explanation. The Handler must account fully for their time spent with a source in the contact note. If Handlers have spent an hour with a source just writing 'social chat' in a contact note will not suffice. Where meetings have been audio recorded, there will not be the same requirement to include such depth of detail. Handlers should not omit anything just because it does not fit with what they believe or with what is generally thought to be correct. We submit what the source tells us and if we don't believe it, we say so and we say why. However, some things are true, whether we believe them or not. Sometimes the source is right and everyone else is wrong.

A clear distinction must be drawn concerning any ***commentary and interpretation.*** Commentary and interpretation help particularly when it is coming from the source. However, if it is not clearly identified it is easy for facts and commentary to merge.

Information submissions should contain a clear indication as to the ***provenance*** of the content. If a source was heard or saw something themselves, this should be indicated in a comment beneath the information. This assists the Intelligence Unit in evaluating the information. Provenance is NOT included in intelligence reports.

Everyone involved has a limited amount of time, therefore **_brevity and clarity_** are important. Avoid unnecessary words, use simple sentences, and understandable language. Good grammar and proper punctuation can help the reader. This is why one Handler writes, and the other checks what has been written.

However, all source reporting should remain **_faithful_** to the words used by the source. There is a tendency to replace the source's words with more formalized language or police jargon. Often this distorts the meaning. For example, the source may say: 'Joe says it is kicking off this Tuesday'. The Handler may write. 'This activity will begin this Tuesday.' Those two statements are not the same. This type of distortion can more easily occur when the source or Handler is not conversing in their mother-tongue. Allowances must be made for things being lost in translation.

It can help the reader if events are put in **_chronological order_**. Although the source may have told things in an order that they recalled it, it is for the Handler to present the information in a way that makes it easier to understand. If the source has reported a linked series of events it can be useful for an analyst to prepare a timeline charting each of the events. For example, if the source has recalled the build-up to a drug shipment, they may speak about when they first heard of it and what happened after that, but they may also speak of what had happened before their first knowledge, of things they found out later. It is very easy for the reader to get confused.

If the information is ***new from the source*** it must be submitted. There is a tendency to omit material that the Handler already knows. They may have heard it from a different source, or it may be common knowledge with those involved in a particular investigation. However, if this is the first time that this source is telling it, it should be submitted. This is for two main reasons. First, it goes to establishing the credibility of the source. They are providing information that can be verified as being correct. The more times the source can be shown as having been truthful, the greater degree of credibility they have. This credibility provides a strong indicator that future information, for which there is no other source, is likely to be true. Second, it provides corroboration of the original information and the original information provides corroboration of what the source is now saying. One corroborates the other. If we want to use this information, for example, to get a warrant, we are always working to corroborate any given piece of information, using other sources of information.

Creating intelligence reports

It is good practice for the Handler to create the draft intelligence reports. They are best positioned to structure the reports in a way that protects the source, while at the same time ensuring that the maximum

245

benefit is gained for the agency. One debrief of a source may produce many different intelligence reports. The Intelligence Unit is in the best position to evaluate the intelligence as they have sight of all the other intelligence coming into the agency. Where there is a dispute over the content of an intelligence report or the content is ambiguous, then discussion should take place between the Intelligence Unit and the Controller so an agreement can be reached about the final product. Having draft intelligence reports to work from, saves everyone involved a lot of time, and produces better reports.

Sanitizing information

Sanitization is the practice of removing or altering the content of a document to protect sensitive sources and/or methodology. Sanitization puts it in a form appropriate for dissemination If intelligence is to be of any use it must be shared, even if there are risks involved with sharing it. Sanitization is a control measure to reduce the risks of sharing intelligence. Sanitization is not an easy task to achieve. It involves significant thought and for want of a better word guile, to remove all traces of where and how intelligence has originated, without losing content, accuracy, and the essence of what was originally reported. Additionally, care must be taken with sanitization to avoid creating ambiguity for those using the intelligence. Ambiguity has the potential to cause serious harm in an investigation. Sanitization is best done by the Handler as they are closest to the raw information and have an in-depth knowledge of its provenance. They also know the risks to the source and how easily they may be exposed. Sanitization can be achieved using several techniques.

Editing involves the removal of certain words or sentences and it is the most common technique used in sanitization. For example: 'Source states...' The intelligence is obviously from a human source. Edit the two words and leave only what they have stated. 'Source states his brother...' In this case, it is not too difficult to work out that it is a human source and who they are. Edit all and leave only the text.

Language modification is about changing words to obscure the origin without obscuring meaning. Often the language used in an information submission will make it apparent where the information has originated. By modifying the words used, the origin becomes vaguer. 'Jack Thompson called his brother to say...' Either the source is the brother, or the information is from an intercept. Change to 'Jack Thompson told his brother ...' To reiterate, care must always be taken that changing the language used by the source may change the meaning.

The ***separation*** of the information into two or more intelligence reports, even though it addresses the same subject matter. Note, where an information submission contains reporting on several subjects. These should, as a matter of course, be separated into individual intelligence reports. This reduces the risk of exposing the origin of the content as collectively the origin may be very apparent.

While it is the responsibility of the Intelligence Unit to ensure that all intelligence has been properly sanitized before it is reposited, there is a real incentive for the Handler to make sure it is done properly. If intelligence is shared that might compromise a source, it is all but impossible to retain control of it.

Evaluating intelligence

Many officers struggle with understanding the concept of evaluating intelligence. They get tied into answering the question: 'Is this from a reliable source?' The question here is focussing on one thing, the source of the information. A more accurate question is: 'Why should we believe *this source* about *this thing*?' The question here focusses on two elements, the source and the specific piece of information. We will now describe how we can answer that question with an abundance of evidence. First, as we have already discussed, the intelligence that we use is not the same as the information we have received from the source. The information we receive is raw and untouched. The intelligence we use has gone through a rigid independent process to ensure its accuracy. During this process, there is a systematic evaluation by trained officers against an agreed set of values. These standardized values are documented and can be presented to whoever needs to see them. The method we advocate is based on what is sometimes referred to as the 'Admiralty Code' or 'Admiralty System'. This system is used by the North Atlantic Treaty Organization (NATO) members to evaluate intelligence.

For those familiar with the Admiralty System and for many in law enforcement, it will be noted that in the assessment that follows we don't use the word reliability when discussing the source. This is deliberate. The meaning of the word reliability, as taken from the Merriam Webster dictionary is *'the quality or state of being reliable'* and when we look at the word *'reliable'* we find *'suitable or fit to be relied on: dependable.'* Where the confusion often arises, and some would say that with defense lawyers is deliberately manufactured, is to associate the reliable/reliability with the individual's character, as opposed to their record regarding the information they have supplied. The argument is made as that this person is 'unreliable' i.e. cannot be depended upon in some way, then anything they say cannot be true. The individual's character is conflated with what they are saying. The generalization is made that all the information coming from them is therefore unreliable. The arguments go a bit like this:

He is a drunk (character) so he cannot be believed (generalization).

She is a thief (character) so everything she will say is dishonest (generalization).

By this means the value of the intelligence is undermined and anything that has been gained from it,

249

is also thrown aside. Given that a huge number of sources have dubious pasts and lead chaotic lives, it is not difficult to support the argument that they are unreliable and should not be believed. Every Handler starts with this suspicion, the difference being that a Handler is trained to make an objective assessment, over time, as opposed to an emotion-driven knee-jerk response. Having explained why we do not use reliable/reliability, we will now explain the terms we do use.

The evaluation of intelligence comprises two elements. First is the ***credibility*** of the origin of the intelligence, in this case, a human source, and second, the ***validity*** of the particular piece of intelligence under discussion. When these two elements are combined, we can arrive at the ***worth of the product***. This is illustrated in Figure 6.1 below, and though shown as an equation it should not be regarded as being mathematical. This formula combing the two elements can be used to assess intelligence coming from any origin, for example surveillance, intercepted communications, etc. Here we will focus on its use concerning human sources.

Figure 6.1 Product Worth

We will now examine what we mean by the two terms credibility and validity and how we arrive at their values.

Credibility

The Merriam Webster dictionary defines credibility as:

'the quality or power of inspiring belief'

When we discuss the credibility of a source, what we are talking about is the reasons we have to believe them. What have they done to make us accept what they are telling us is the truth? The main element here will always be their track record. If they have continually told us things that have been confirmed as being true, then their credibility score is going to be high. If some things they say are proven correct and others proved wrong, then we are going to be a bit more dubious and score their credibility accordingly. If we don't know, we are going to say we don't know. Most of a source's early reporting will have a score that reflects our lack of certainty about them.

There are some other factors we will wish to consider in arriving at our grade for credibility. Is there consistency/inconsistency with the information provided on previous occasions and what is now being reported? One week they say one thing and *without explanation,* their account changes the following week.

We must always consider the partiality of the source. Many sources will taint information to address their agenda, for their benefit, or to cause harm to someone else. We must always question the motive of the source to provide each piece of information. Too often Handlers think that because there is a huge motive for

251

the source to talk to them, that this correlates with always being truthful to them. Handlers need to think about what is motivating the source. This again assumes that the evaluating member has a proper understanding of human motivation. Often, they don't.[14]

Grade	Credibility	Explanation	Spontaneous interpretation
A	Completely credible	There is no doubt regarding authenticity or competence of this source. The source has a prolonged history of being credible.	Gets it right all the time.
B	Usually credible	Source has a history of credibility having been incorrect on only one or two occasions during a prolonged period.	Right more often than not.
C	Fairly credible	Source has a history of being correct much more often than they are incorrect, but some of their reporting has been inaccurate.	Take a bit of time to be sure.
D	Usually not credible	The source has supplied some information in the past that has been incorrect or unacceptably inaccurate.	Read it but don't put a lot of faith in what is said.
E	Untrustworthy	There are serious concerns about the source. The source may have a history of providing false or misleading information or is strongly suspected of doing so.	Danger. Be careful this individual has the potential to cause harm.
F	Cannot be judged	The source cannot be judged. This grading will be used when there is no or little history of providing information.	We don't know.

Table 6.1 Credibility Values

Handlers are often reluctant to use the 'A' grade 'just in case' on this occasion the source is wrong. That is a flawed way of thinking. Similarly, they are reluctant to use the 'F' grade with a new source. They think it will

---

[14] For a better understanding of Motivation. See book: 'Why - Understanding Motive and Motivation'

undermine the source from the beginning or because they want to use the information straight away. This defeats the purpose of the evaluation and over the long-term, undermines the whole system. Where there has been repeated intentional deceit the grading for credibility will be 'E', Similarly, if the source is particularly manipulative, seeking to use the agency for their gains this may be an appropriate grade. On the other hand, just because a person is being manipulative does not mean what they are saying is untrue. What we are trying to indicate to the end-user is: 'Take care if you are going to use this intelligence.'

When it comes to credibility the question we have to answer is:

'Why do you believe this source?'

If we want to use this intelligence our answer to this should be 'because the source consistently provides intelligence that has been independently verified.' We now move on to the validity of the information.

Validity

The Miriam Webster dictionary defines Validity as:

'the quality or state of being valid: such as

a: the state of being acceptable according to the law
b: the quality of being well-grounded, sound, or correct.'

Validity refers to the believability of a specific piece of intelligence that has been provided. Important in the definition above is the element that something that is valid is 'acceptable according to law'. This is what we are trying to achieve. As part of the process of turning information into intelligence, each separate piece of information is assessed for validity regardless of it being presented to the agency, at the same time, from the same source, like many other pieces of information. This is because the source will often have obtained the information in different ways and under differing circumstances. Each of these factors is likely to affect the validity of the information. The provenance of the information is often critical in assessing its validity. This is why the Handler should make an initial assessment of its validity. The Handler knows how the source came by it. Where there is a doubt, there should be no hindrance to the Intelligence Unit liaising with the Handler to discuss the provenance of a piece of information.

Factors to consider when assessing the validity of the information provided include: How does this piece of information fit with what is already known? For the most part, there will be other intelligence available that supports or contradicts what is being said by the source. It does not have to be exactly the same to support it. For example, the source may say 'Billy Baxter has bought a new car. It is a BMW.' Surveillance may have observed Baxter driving a red BMW the previous day. The information from surveillance corroborates the information from the source. Although the core of the information may be impossible to verify, the parts surrounding it may be verifiable by other means. If parts of it are true, there is a better chance that it as a whole is true, than if no part can be verified. Similarly, if there is information to contradict what the source has said, this may raise a discussion as to which piece of information is correct, or more likely to be correct.

Another aspect that we will use is the analysis of the information itself, including its meaning and structure. Are details missing that should be there if the information was true? Does it make sense, in and of itself? Do the timelines make sense? Care must be taken that these omissions are not due to the incompetence of the Handler. A lot of the time, incomplete reporting is down to the Handler not exploring the information in-depth, and not down to any deception or deliberate omission, on the part of the source.

The Handler should also pay attention to the placement of the source within the group on which they are reporting. Would they have been in a position to hear such material directly?

A useful tool in deciding validity is 'the criterion of multiple attestations'. This tool is often used by Biblical scholars to help determine the validity of actions or sayings attributed to Jesus. While many actions of Jesus may be supported through other passages of the New Testament, scholars also look to other writings such as noncanonical sources, to authenticate what is written in the New Testament. The principles used are similar to what we can use in assessing the validity of what the source is saying. For example, we can look at what we are hearing on intercepts or what surveillance is reporting. The criterion of multiple attestations states that when two or more independent sources present similar or consistent accounts, it is more likely that the accounts are accurate. To put it simply, the more consistent reports we have of an event, the greater the validity value will be, concerning what this source has said.

Where information comes to a source 'second-hand', the validity grading will always start from a lower position. This does not mean that we will not believe what the source is saying, they may be being as truthful as they can be about what they have heard. However, the person that told them may be of limited capacity, or they may have a reason to lie to the source, or they may be merely repeating what they have heard. The Handler will need to explore the circumstances leading up to when the source was told, We should seek the source's opinion as to why the other person may have told them. Second-hand information is like second-hand everything. We need to accept that it is not as perfect as we want it to be and it may be all we have but it is a lot better than having nothing at all.

Grade	Validity	Explanation	Spontaneous Interpretation
1	Confirmed	Other independent reports have confirmed the content. It is logical in itself and is corroborated by other existing intelligence on the subject.	This is true.
2	Probably true	Although the content has not been confirmed independently, it is logical in itself and agrees with other existing intelligence on the subject.	More than likely true.
3	Possibly true	Although the content has not been confirmed it is reasonably logical in itself and it is, in at least part, supported by other intelligence on the subject.	Not sure. Calls for judgement in action.
4	Of doubtful truth	The content is unconfirmed and while not illogical it is assessed as being incorrect. The information is not believed at time of evaluation, but it remains possible that it is true.	Not true
5	Believed to be false	There is reliable intelligence available that contradicts the content. It appears illogical in itself. The manner or circumstances in which it was reported gives strong indications that it is false.	False. Handle with care
6	Cannot be judged	There is insufficient knowledge to make a judgement on the validity of the information.	No idea

Table 6.2 Validity Values

When it comes to validity the question we have to answer is:

'Why do you believe this piece of intelligence?'

If we want to use this intelligence our answer should be 'because there are five other similar pieces of intelligence that support, it and all our investigations verify it as far as is reasonably practical.'

Reliability

Returning to our formula in Figure 6.1, we will now examine how this formula provides a clear indication as to the *reliability* of the intelligence. Reliability is central to the utilization of the intelligence where the agency wishes to obtain warrants based upon it. Another way of expressing the product's worth is to say if it is reliable or not. Returning to our definition we are trying to establish if the product is 'suitable or fit to be relied on: dependable.'

When using this formula to arrive at the product worth the guiding principle is that *any intelligence report that has a value of A1, A2, B1, or B2, has sufficient worth to be viewed as* **reliable**. Legally speaking, it is worthy of confidence and is sufficient to obtain a warrant.

This grading establishes the credibility of the source, the need for corroboration, and the need for independent investigation of the content. Ideally, when requesting a warrant, the Investigator would present to the court several similarly graded intelligence reports with each one corroborating the other. These documents may originate in a variety of ways such as surveillance, or intercept, and/or from a number of different human sources. All intelligence reports should be in a similar format. Just because a piece of intelligence is graded below these four grades does not in and of itself make it useless. It just means that we have to be more circumspect in using it.

This method of evaluating intelligence creates a double-lock. The initial lock is that the human source is independently graded against the different grades. If circumstances exist where only the Handler of the source makes this grading the Handler is limited by their knowledge and they or most likely to be prejudiced in favor of what 'their source' says. For the naïve, and inexperienced manager it should be noted that Handler and source performance, are intrinsically linked. If the source is being deceitful then the Handler must be a fool not to see that. The Handler's professional credibility is tied to that of the source and the Handler risks losing their objectivity. They have a vested interest in saying the source is credible. Furthermore, if they want a particular search carried out there is a huge incentive to say the source is credible. Assessment of their performance is related to the source being believed.

When the assessment of the source is done through an independent process the risk of this happening is all but eliminated because so many checks are in place. First, the Handler is well-trained and is aware of the potential for such biases and knows that they have support in making judgments on the credibility of the source. Second, the Controller monitors the source relationship, continually assessing the credibility of the source. Third, the final assessment of the source's credibility is made independent of the source management team, in the Intelligence Unit. They have no incentive to be more or less critical in their judgment.

The second lock is that each separate piece of information is assessed in a similar way, against a different set of values. The Handler will explore the provenance of each piece of information with the source. The Controller will verify that the Handler has done this before forwarding it to the Intelligence Unit. The Intelligence Unit can analyze any new piece of information against all existing intelligence held by the agency. They can see if it is corroborated by other intelligence or conflicts with other intelligence.

All the processes outlined in this book contribute towards ensuring the production of great amounts of more accurate intelligence. With these processes, the end-user can have much greater confidence in the grading attached to the intelligence. It has been created by well-trained officers working in an integrated system, that has been designed to increase accuracy. An alternative is an untrained officer taking information from a source, that no one else knows about, and then presenting that information to a court and stating under oath that it is reliable.

Warrants

This is not a law book, but what we are trying to do is to provide Handlers with the knowledge that is contextually embedded. Fortunately, while each country has nuances when it comes to the law, the general principles are sufficiently similar to allow for discussion. The first thing that needs to be said is that if an Investigator knows the identity of a source, they risk telling it to the 'court'. Once the court knows, the agency has lost control of where it goes. If a judge **needs** to know the source identity this should be done only under exceptional circumstances, and only to the judge.

Second, all too often the discussion is around the personal traits of the source, or on the number of pieces of information that the one specific source has previously provided. Where there is only one source providing the information and there have been no, or only, limited steps are taken to corroborate the information during analysis, the value of the intelligence produced will always be questionable.

Third, too often the go-to way of corroborating a source is to send the source to a drug dealer's house to buy drugs under 'controlled circumstances'. This has flaws, the foremost being it puts the source directly in the evidential chain. It becomes very difficult to protect them in the disclosure process and creates unnecessary risk for the source. (We will discuss buy/bust operations in detail later.)

In many cases, the problem with convincing a court to issue a warrant arises because of poor intelligence management. First, agencies don't know the difference between information and intelligence and don't have structures in place to separate the two. What is often presented to the court is raw information and not evaluated intelligence. Second, when Investigators want to obtain a warrant, the affidavit does not provide sufficient cause to justify the warrant. This is because there is no process to establish the reliability of the material contained in the affidavit or the Investigator cannot articulate the process and the safeguards involved in it, to the court. Third, because many judges do not understand intelligence, they focus on the question: 'Is your informant reliable?' As we have established, this is a deeply flawed question. The questions should be: Is the intelligence you are presenting to the court reliable? Is it sufficient to establish reasonable suspicion/probable cause? Whatever the standard is that the court requires to issue a warrant, the Investigator must be able to prove the standard is met. If it is not properly established at the time the warrant is issued, then one can be certain it will be examined by the defense, in any subsequent prosecution.

When accompanying the affidavit a properly created intelligence report does not identify the *origin* of the information contained in it. It contains a grading of the credibility of where the information has come from and an assessment of the validity of the information – two values. This meets the legal standards required in many jurisdictions. For example, in the USA, the most common ways of establishing reliability are by showing that 'it is corroborated by other evidence, or [that] the confidential informant has a history of providing reliable information.'[15]. Validity is about ensuring there is supporting evidence and credibility is about the source's history. Another key criterion that has been raised by courts is the need for the intelligence to be

---

[15] United States v. Butler, 594 F.3d 955 (8th Cir. 2010)

'independently investigated'. This criterion is satisfied by the independent analysis by the Intelligence Unit. All these factors add to the 'totality of circumstances'[16] that the court must consider in granting a warrant.

Using intelligence reports for warrants eliminates the specific need to state the origin of the information (i.e. the source) Common errors made concerning warrants are many. First, In the affidavit, the Investigator writes something akin to 'confidential informant 165, went to the 267 Bay Street on Friday 5th of July and purchased drugs.' There may have only been one visitor to the house on that day: It makes it very easy to identify the source. Furthermore, by stating the identity number of the source (165) it opens up that source for further scrutiny, now or later, in court or in the criminal fraternity. Second, the Investigator uses a code name for the source that gives clues as to their identity or that is derogatory: 'Bill the baker' – the source works in a bakery; 'Fat Fred' – the source is large in stature; 'Mary' - the source is female. Third, the Investigator gets bogged down in details about the source's traits: lazy, always late, drinks heavily, etc. as opposed to speaking as to the credibility of the information they have given in the past. A source can be lazy and tardy and a heavy drinker, but they may have a long history of always giving accurate information. Investigators often confuse what they are assessing. It is not the person. It is their history with giving information.

---

[16] Illinois v. Gates, 462 U.S. 213 (1983)

To make this clear if an officer wants to search 267, Bay Street, Tintown, the home of a drug dealer Victor Hopping, what they should present to the court are numerous intelligence reports, all of which are evaluated with high grades (A1-B2). These should read:

> *'High-grade intelligence states that Victor Hopping is selling illegal drugs, including crystal and cocaine. He uses 267, Bay Street, Tintown, in connection with this activity.'*

The more reports there are and the greater detail in them, the more corroboration there is that the activity is taking place, as alleged. Then a court is more likely to be satisfied that the warrant can be justified. What the Investigator is trying to establish is that the information is sufficient to satisfy a 'prudent person's belief.'

As we have previously stated intelligence reports should all be anonymized so that no one can tell if they came from a human source, a telephone intercept, or an undercover officer. The judge should issue a warrant based on the value of the intelligence presented and not solely on the word of one officer saying their source is 'reliable'.

It is recognized that some may see the presentation of intelligence reports without discussion of the origin of the content as a fundamental change in how business is carried out. However, it isn't. It is meeting the standards that courts expect in a way that is safer for all concerned. This way just takes a bit more

264

explanation, to begin with. It is akin to when we used to allow people to work on a building site without hard hats. They could do it, but some people got hurt, unnecessarily. The method here satisfies the requirements of the courts to a higher standard, and it affords greater protection to the source. It is a win, win.

Changing the grade

Just because something did not appear true at the time the information was obtained does not mean that it is not true. If it is proved true later the grading should be changed accordingly. If this piece of information has harmed the subsequent grading of the credibility of the source, it is worth making a note in the source decision log of what has occurred. It may be necessary to re-evaluate some of the intelligence from the point they were suspected erroneously of being deceitful. However, any evaluation is generally based on what is known at the relevant time so revaluation will be the exception rather than the rule. And of course, if the source is found to have deliberately lied about some information, a similar course of action may have to be taken. The greatest risk here is that such a revelation may put in jeopardy warrants previously obtained using the source's information.

Dissemination

There is no point in collecting information unless it is useful to someone. Choosing the right level of dissemination is not easy. Too high a level and those that should see it can't and too low a level and we risk compromising the source. One solution is to initially err on the side of caution and place a higher, more restrictive, dissemination level to commence with and then after a time, review it, with the potential to share it more widely upon review. Ultimately, it is the decision of the Intelligence Unit as to whom an intelligence report is disseminated and under what conditions it is shared. Recall, before being disseminated all intelligence is first lodged in the agency's intelligence repository where those with an appropriate access level can automatically read it. Intelligence should be disseminated to those who can make use of it. Where there is an expectation that action will be taken immediately or within a reasonable period, it should be indicated that the intelligence is being disseminated 'for action'.

Where the dissemination of a particular piece of intelligence is likely to place the life of the source in imminent danger the Authorizing Officer must be informed, prior to the intelligence being disseminated. The Authorizing Officer should liaise with the officer in charge of the Intelligence Unit and discuss alternatives. In cases where agreement cannot be reached, it will be for the Senior Responsible Officer to decide if the intelligence is disseminated or not.

If intelligence is being disseminated to another agency, no indications should be given that it has come from a human source. Also, while requests can be made that it be handled in a particular way, it cannot be assumed that it will be. The recipient agency will do with it what it thinks best, for that agency.

Collection to Exploitation

To recap, there is no point in collecting information unless we turn it into intelligence that is of use to the agency. Our goal in this process is always to increase the quantity and quality of the intelligence produced. The process we have now produces intelligence that it is safe to use. The raw information has been put through a process that reduces the potential for cognitive biases and individual errors to degrade the information. What we have is a process that will stand up to any judicial scrutiny and that produces intelligence of a standard required by any court.

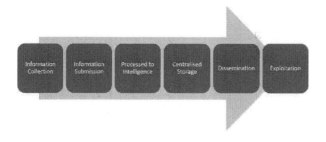

Figure 6.2 Collection to Exploitation

The six steps that ensure the integrity in exploiting intelligence from human sources.

1. Collected by a trained Handler who is independent of the investigation.

2. Submitted through a Controller for quality assurance.
3. Independently processed and evaluated by trained officers against an agreed set of values.
4. Stored in a central repository where the original cannot be altered.
5. Disseminated to the Investigator who decides what they want to do with it based on the independent evaluation.
6. The exploitation of the intelligence in an accountable way.

As can be seen, the information must pass through the hands of many trained professionals before it can be used. At each step, the officer involved is accountable for their actions and the entire process is documented. This negates the risk of an officer using information for personal or professional advancement. It protects the rights of citizens and protects the life of the source.

Conclusion

Now that we understand the nature of memory, and how to conduct a debrief, and how to turn the information into intelligence, we should all be fairly confident we can do the job... Except that our minds are still limited by what we have experienced. There are many things that, had we been thinking, or had we more experience, we maybe should have asked.

7. Widening the View

*Albert grunted. "Do you know what happens to lads who ask
too many questions?"
Mort thought for a moment.
"No," he said eventually, "what?"
There was silence.
Then Albert straightened up and said, "Damned if I know.
Probably they get answers and serve 'em right."*

Mort - Terry Pratchett

Introduction

I would not blame you if you are tempted to skip this
chapter. It is pretty much made up of a list of
questions. In truth, I was tempted to skip writing it. I
had two reasons. First, I pretty much assumed it would
be skipped, and second, some days it is just hard to
keep putting the effort in. We all want to get better but
sometimes it just seems too much like hard work. Why
bother if no one else will notice either way?
Professional Handlers know why.

I read through the notes I have made, for this chapter
and I realized I started the list over twenty years ago
and I began it because I realized there were a lot of
things that I never even thought of asking a source.
What is included here is a list of both general topics
and specific questions to go through with a source.
They are intended to open the mind of the Handler to
other topics that the source may be able to provide

information on. Even if the source does not have any specific information on the topics raised, they can act as a catalyst in the activation of other memories. Many of these questions the experienced Handler may well be aware of but have let slip from their mind. With others, they may be just an idea to run past the source on a day when there is not much else going on. Sometimes we can be surprised by just how much the source knows.

Questions galore

If a source is to reach their full potential the Handler must attempt to extract the maximum amount of information from the source. One of the most effective ways to do this is for the Handler to ask questions about topics that don't normally arise in conversations with the source, However, the extent to which a Handler can do this is often limited by both their knowledge of what is potentially of interest to the agency and their knowledge of the information to which the source may have access. In this chapter, we explore many different business areas and make suggestions as to the types of questions a Handler may wish to ask. Common sense will often dictate whether or not there is any point in asking a particular source a particular group of questions. Furthermore, early exploration of the source's background and completion of the enhanced profile (see Chapter 3 on Enhanced Profiling) will indicate if the source is likely to be able to be tasked into situations where they may be able to obtain the required information.

270

Some of the answers obtained may have limited use in addressing specific intelligence requirements or be useful only to a limited number of officers or sections within the agency. Some questions may appear to be extremely basic. However, circumstances change, and it is incumbent upon the Handler to keep the agency's intelligence systems up to date. For example, a local bar frequented by criminals may change ownership or may have a nickname that is used by a particular criminal gang in which the agency has an interest. Thus, recapping the names of local bars with a source has both relevance and utility. Many times, a source will not tell us things because in their world everyone knows these things and they assume that we will already know.

Many of the questions contained here do not need to be asked by direct questioning. The answers will often come through prolonged periods spent conversing with the source, with the various topics being raised and the source encouraged to expand on what they know.

There are a few points to bear in mind. There is little point in the Handler acquiring this information if they are not prepared to write it up afterward. Answering many of these questions encourages the source to speak freely about topics that they may not even know the Handler is interested in. If they go off track, allow them to follow the path their memories are taking them on. When a source is giving information do not discourage them, they may begin to enjoy it. Another thing to remember is that nothing in this life comes for free. If the source has provided a lot of information we want, they should be rewarded for it. Pay them for their time and their knowledge.

Subject specialists

While most Handlers will have a very good knowledge of most crime types, there are some very specialist types of crime where specialist knowledge is needed, for example, money laundering, computer crime, and pedophilia. Where a source is reporting on such matters it is useful to bring a subject specialist with specific knowledge of this offending, to some debriefs. They should be introduced to the source as such, unless there is doubt about the credibility of the source. The Handler will continue to take the lead regarding security and the relationship, allowing the subject specialist the freedom to debrief the source. If the source is likely to be reporting on the topic in question for a prolonged period, then the specialist will need training at least to Level 2 (See Chapter 2)

Questioning risks

Before commencing to question a source there is one more thing to bear in mind and that is that the mere fact of a Handler asking a question conveys information to the source and creates risks. First, it tells the source that the Handler has an interest in the topic. The more detailed the questioning, the greater the interest and potentially the greater worth in any information that is provided. Second, it tells the source that the Handler does not know the information. This may convey to the source a lack of knowledge and an opportunity for the source to be make up information. Third, the Handler may compromise other sources. If the Handler asks about a person called Paul, who is not well known, the source may start to investigate how the Handler knew about Paul.

We will now look at the various topics we may want to discuss with a source. Each Handler will have their style and know the best way to open up such topics with the source. While much of it should come through normal conversation this assumes that the Handler has the prerequisite level of interpersonal skills.

Included here are several tables with suggested themes for questions. Rather than going into a detailed explanation of what is meant by each particular question, they are intended here to make the Handler think about potential avenues for obtaining greater information. Avoid the temptation to dismiss them as 'things that we already know' or as 'things that the source would never know'.

Biographical information

Biographic information refers to information about any person. To comply with civil liberty and human rights legislation we must be able to justify why we are collecting and retaining information about any person. The authorization process ensures that there is justification for the collection and having that information processed through the Intelligence Unit ensures that there is independent review as to whether or not it should be retained. Furthermore, all intelligence reports should be reviewed after an identified period to see if there remains a justification for keeping those records. We collect information on people of actual or potential importance. The more closely tied a person is to involvement in criminality the greater the justification for keeping the intelligence on them.

For example, if a source is reporting on the comings and goings, from a house where drug dealing is taking place and they see a person visit on five separate occasions, there is going to be suspiciously about that person, so we would retain the intelligence. However, if the person arrives in a plumber's van enters with tools and emerges an hour later, the long-term retention of the information would be more difficult to justify and should be destroyed.

When it comes to the sort of information we want to collect on a person suspected of being involved in crime, the rule of thumb will be, the more serious the crime, the greater their involvement, then the greater amount of information we should be collecting on that person. For example, with a member of the Mafia then everything we can find out is important.

Biographical Information	
Personal	**Addresses**
Full names (written in their language). Nicknames (if widely known or not). Aliases. Family (relationships with each). Description. Personality. Likes and dislikes. Hobbies. Languages spoken Faith. Friends and associates.	Home address. Work address. City of origin. Other properties, owned, etc. Places frequented.
	Patterns of life
	Daily routine. Idiosyncrasies, habits, mannerisms and unusual lifestyles.
Finances	**Criminality**
Education. Employment history. Sources of income. Bank details. Spending habits.	Position in organisation. Duration of involvement. Prison History. Propensity for violence. Addictions. Specialist skills.

Table 7.1 Biographical Information

Social and cultural information

Occasionally a Handler may know the area they are working in well. They may have grown up in the area or been a long-term resident. However, even in this case, there were will be parts of the society from which they are removed. For most Handlers, their knowledge of the area will be professional. Many large cities will have areas and populations that are removed from, if not openly hostile to, law enforcement. In smaller towns, there will be parts of society in which law enforcement has limited insight. Sources move in different circles and they are often connected with parts of society that are hard for law enforcement to reach.

Another aspect to be remembered is that each source is a resource for the entire agency. Currently, many officers only task sources to gain information about what their particular unit requires. Dedicated Source Units serve all in the agency.

At a strategic level, there is always a need for the Chief of Police or Commissioner to know how particular sections of the community feel about ongoing events. While politicians will be in regular contact, their actions will often be self-promoting, and they will be pushing their agenda. It is beneficial for a Chief to be able to access the thoughts and feelings of the local community and some sources can provide this. The same can be said about Dedicated Source Units serving their local Area-Commander.

One issue that can use a lot of law enforcement resources is addressing public order issues including protests. Knowing if there is the potential for the protest to turn violent allows a Chief to police it more effectively and keep everyone safer. Tasking sources to attend such activities can pay dividends especially if they can forewarn of potential violence. Equally, it can also save money, where the source can predict that violence is unlikely to occur, reducing the need for a heavy and potentially antagonistic looking, police presence. Sources can provide useful information to help crime prevention. Many sources know how they commit crimes. We can take this knowledge and use it against other criminals. The source can say what prevention strategies deterred them and which ones were useful. This is all valuable information when we are trying to lower crime rates.

Social and Cultural Information	
Community Attitudes	**Cultural Norms**
How are these people viewed in their community? Why? What type of behavior annoys the community? How are the police viewed? Who is respected in the community? Names of community leaders. Community thoughts on historic events.	What is the ethnic make up of neighbourhood? What languages are spoken? Are the significant times within the community? (Social and relating to criminality.) What is the economic make up of the community? Are there cultural norms that constrain the organization?
Local knowledge	**Community interaction**
Local names of bars, cafes, etc. Landmarks. Focal and rendezvous points. Places of worship. Scrap dealers, second-hand stores, etc.	Is there an awareness in the community of ongoing criminal activity? Is there a pattern? Is there a build up? Public order issues. Protest.

Table 7.2 Social and Cultural Information

When it comes to generating conversation with a source about a particular area, maps or aerial photography can be useful tools. As we discussed earlier, they may assist the source in remembering details, but they may also assist in bringing to mind previously unmentioned elements that are of interest. Where a Handler is unfamiliar with area maps are essential. Fortunately, they are now readily on hand on a smartphone or tablet.

Organized crime information

Many sources report on organized crime. Unfortunately, much of the reporting tends to be tactical information. If all that is done is tackle organized crime at a tactical level nothing really changes. The organization just keeps going, despite losing a few foot soldiers along the way. To cause real harm, organized crime gangs need to be attacked at all levels in all ways. While there is some legitimacy in the argument that if we remove one gang, they are rapidly replaced by another, the next gang may lack experience and may not function as well. Like any business replacing experienced people is not always easy and less experienced ones make more mistakes.

Sources should be questioned about all gangs operating in their area regardless of size. There can be a tendency to think of organized crime almost exclusively in terms of large organizations. If there is to be a sustainable campaign against criminal gangs, we must be able to identify all the players and emerging threats.

Organized Crime Information	
Structure	**Business areas**
What is the hierarchy? What separate groupings are there? Number of members. How is the structured adhered to ? What specialist roles are there? Is there a long-term strategy? In what ways is the organization vulnerable? (For example, anti-racketeering laws.) Who would take over the roles of the key personalities if they are removed? Does the gang use tattoos for members? Do they have tags to mark territory?	What are all the types of criminality they are involved in? How is business divided up? Is there any subcontracting / franchising? What links does the organization have to legitimate businesses? What manufacturing processes are the organization involved in? (Drug production, etc.) What are the logistics and supply chains? Are they involved counterfeiting goods?
Geographical spread	**Weapons**
What areas does the gang operate in? Do they have connections elsewhere? How were these connections made? How strong are they? How often do the parties meet?	What type of weapons do they have access to? Where do they keep them? Do they have access to explosives/knowledge of explosives? How are these procured?
Transport	**Morale**
What vehicles are at the groups disposal? How do they arrange international travel? How do they move illicit goods? What would disrupt these supply routes?	Is there dissension in the organization? How cohesive is the organization? Is their factional infighting?

Table 7.3 Organized crime information

Terrorism and national security

The term 'terrorism and national security' is intended to incorporate all threats emanating from extremist groups, regardless of their political leanings. Care must be taken in identifying what is a legitimate political activity and where it crosses to potentially unlawful activity. Where there is doubt authorization for a source to report on such matters, should always go to the Senior Responsible Officer.

Terrorism and National Security Information	
Political	**Faith-Based**
What are the desired end goals? Where does the power lie within organisation? What strategies are they employing? What do they see as the government vulnerabilities? Who is responsible for propaganda? What means do they use? What notable successes do they believe they have had? What government counter-initiatives do they view as problematic? Who decides the targets?	What doctrine is adhered to? Who are the revered religious leaders What religious leaders are despised? How does the community view their activities? Who opposes their end goals and/or their tactics?
Subversion	**International support**
Have they penetrated community groups? What are they using these groups for? Do they have contacts in mainstream media? What media outlets does the group view as supporting their cause? Are there any links to government officials?	What international connections are their? How do they communicate with these people? Is their state backed support?
Recruitment	**Finance**
Is there a structured recruitment process? Where are new members recruited from and how? Is there any group they feel are more vulnerable for recruitment? Are their any particular type they want to recruit? What excludes someone from joining?	Where does the group get their money? What do they spend the money on? What currencies do they use? (Bitcoin? etc.) Who is involved with the money? How much do they have?

Table 7.4 Terrorism and national security

Some sources may not be in a position to report on matters about terrorism or national security. However, there is often a crossover and it is worth exploring the issue with the source. Terrorists may seek to procure weapons, explosives, or other logistics from the criminal fraternity and many young people have moved from being involved in criminality to become involved in terrorism. Prisons are also a place where people have been recruited into extremist groups. Handlers should make themselves aware of any potential threats from terrorism or to national security that may be present in their area. Table 7.4 provides some of the topics a Handler may want to raise with a source.

If a source is reporting on these topics any information the source can supply may be important. Where the reporting is a one-off event, the Handler may well need the assistance of a subject specialist to assist in debriefing the source. Where the source is reporting continually on terrorism, they should be managed by Handlers attached to the terrorism command.

Communications information

Criminals need to communicate. How they communicate and the language they use will always be of interest. Sources can provide valuable information to support other covert law enforcement functions. If we want to intercept a telephone, we need to know which phone is the best one to intercept. If we listen to telephones, we need to know what code words are being used. With the advent of the age of information technology, we need to know what methods the criminals are using and how they are using them.

Communications Information	
Phone based	**Language**
What are the numbers of group members? (Source will have many in phone) What 'apps' are used by group? Why? Where do they purchase phones? Which communication links are most worth monitoring?	What language does the group converse in? If they change language does that signify anything? What code words do they use? Are there rules around initiating contact?
Computers	**Alternative means**
What computers do they use? How sophisticated are they? Is there anyone with expertise? What levels of encryption do they have? What email addresses does the source know?	What alternative means of contact do the group use? How do they work? Who is aware to these methods? Do they use radios? What type? Where do they get them?

Table 7.5 Communications Information

There are many crimes committed using the internet and the internet is used to facilitate many crimes. Where we have a source that has detailed knowledge of topics such as hacking, then it is time to bring in a specialist to talk to them. If any source knows how the 'dark web' is being used it is worth involving a specialist. We all like to fool ourselves that we have a 'working knowledge' of these things, but few do.

If the criminals are using specialist equipment, for example, to access computers or bank machines, then we are going to want to get the source to bring us that technology. Similarly, with criminal gangs that use technology to circumvent burglar alarms or car security systems then Handlers need to ask the source about where this equipment is obtained from and can they get it.

A simple way of accessing information, though one which a source may find too intrusive, is to ask them to go through their phone and discuss the people in it. This can be managed by asking them to leave out any 'personal' contacts discussing only those involved in crime. At the same time, Handlers can also obtain the telephone number of suspects contained there.

Money laundering and financial information

The vast majority of crime is carried out for monetary gain. When it comes to organized crime the sums involved can be breath-taking. Understanding how an organization launders its money is critical if we want to damage them. It is fair to say that the methods employed by some gangs are beyond the understanding of most of us. We simply do not have a background in the financial industry, but neither do the criminals and they need to access specialist resources to do this. Any information about how money is being laundered is important and a source who can provide information on the methods employed will be of potential use to many different agencies. Handlers need to maximize the use of subject specialists to gain details of the information and the Intelligence Unit should prepare briefing papers on the methodology being employed and disseminate it to other agencies.

Money laundering is not the only topic relating to finance that will be of interest. Other elements of interest include, how money is split across gang members, how much is paid in bribes and to who, how much profit is made from each commodity, how rents are paid for buildings, or how vehicles are purchased. In the drug trade, the break-down of drug prices at each level of the transaction will be of interest, together with fluctuations in price because of shortages, etc.

Assets are another important issue to enquire about. Many times, the source will assume that law enforcement already knows about a criminal owning property in another country or about the yacht they have moored in some exclusive marina. These are the type of things that can be used in asset seizures or queried under unexplained wealth legislation. Criminals want money and this creates vulnerabilities for them. The greater the knowledge of their finances, the greater the potential to damage their activities.

Sex crimes and human trafficking

While some sources may be directly reporting on sex crimes and human trafficking, others may have some passing knowledge of it. Many sources move in a world that is alien to us and of which even many law enforcement officers have only limited knowledge. For example, 'strip clubs' are places that are often owned or frequented by those involved in crime. A source who frequents such places may hear a lot of what could be called 'the word on the street'. While much of this may be just gossip, some of it can be useful. Similarly, women involved in the sex industry often hear things that others would not. These women talk amongst themselves and often overhear useful information. They are also often victims of unreported crime and can identify people involved in sexual deviancy, which is linked to criminality. While there are specific ethical risks in talking to people associated with the sex industry, on occasions it can be the only place one can find out about what is happening in that section of society. Human trafficking for sexual purposes is a huge problem across the world and gaining information about it is extremely difficult. It is certainly easier and engages less risk, to recruit a source involved in that world already, than to try and place an undercover officer into it.

Talking to a source about such matters may be embarrassing for some officers, while for others it is not unusual to find them obtaining unconscious or unavowed, sexual gratification from such discussions. For the source, there may also be embarrassment about revealing how they have gained the knowledge, while others will revel in the sense of brazenness, they get from it. The Handler needs to adopt a clinical-like approach, and at the same time remaining non-judgmental, for example, concerning sex-workers.

People are often trafficked for forced labor in industries such as construction, agriculture and the food industry. Many of these crimes occur under the radar of normally policing. However, because of areas where sources live or frequent they may become aware of houses were such workers are kept or people who are involved in employing them.

People smuggling

Smuggling people for financial gain has become big business for criminals and is likely to remain so while there is such disparity in wealth between nations. People smuggling differs from human trafficking in that the goal is the transport of a willing person without the exploitation of them at the termination of the journey, though sometimes the lines between trafficking and smuggling blur. Here also sources can potentially supply information. They may have heard rumors of a particular trucking company that is involved or of a local restaurant that sponsors the smuggling of people, who become employees. Because these types of activities are carried out in a clandestine way involving a limited number of perpetrators, any small piece of information can be a vital breakthrough.

Responding to a crime

Crimes happen and sources should always be in a position to respond where they may be able to assist in an investigation. It may be to answer a simple question as to the potential motive for a drive-by shooting or why a person was abducted. Often sources will hear talk about such matters long before the Investigators. Timely information can make a big difference in any investigation. There is no reason why a source cannot be tasked to find out the address of a suspect to aid a uniform officer in their investigation. This saves wasting resources. It also builds the reputation of the Dedicated Source Unit and can lead to uniform officers suggesting potential sources to the Unit. Having said all that care must always be taken that the use of a source in such a way, does not compromise the source or damage the potential for achieving the long-term goals for that source. Although the request may be made informally for assistance the resulting information is always processed through the Intelligence Unit before being provided to the officer concerned.

Corruption

Sources will often have access to information about the corruption of public figures including law enforcement officers. The agency needs to have in place procedures as to how such material is to be handled. Where the information contains an allegation of corruption against a police officer, it may be appropriate for that information to go exclusively to the Internal Affairs department or a designated person within the Intelligence Unit. Obviously, the fewer people that have sight of this type of information, the more likely that an effective investigation can be carried out.

In a similar vein, sources also come across information that relates to illegal or unethical behavior on the part of lawyers. Every citizen is legally entitled to engage the services of a lawyer and most lawyers know where the line is concerning adhering to their ethical standards. However, some cross the line, and their association with criminal clients becomes questionable. With others, they become an integral part of the criminal gang, while at the same time flying under the banner of being an 'official of the court' or some similar flag of convenience. Because of their legal standing and the need to protect the criminal justice system, any information of the criminal involvement of a lawyer must be properly reported. Criminal involvement does not include legitimately defending their client.

For public officials, law enforcement officers, or lawyers, any behavior that leaves them vulnerable to being blackmailed or exploited by a criminal gang will be of interest, particularly where it is known that the criminal gang is aware of the vulnerability. Examples include visiting prostitutes by a police officer, or drug-taking by a court official. In all cases, civil liberty issues will have to be considered regarding the retention of such information or about with whom it can be shared. It is the Handler's job to submit the information and the role of the Intelligence Unit to decide how it is disseminated. This negates any allegations that are made against the Handler concerning spreading rumors, etc.

Salacious tales

Handlers will often hear many stories that circulate within the criminal underworld. The very nature of the people involved, and the nature of the activities that they engage in, means that there are often stories circulating of the personal activities of people known to the source and of whom the Handler has a legitimate. interest. Where a source recants such stories and they are of no intelligence worth, these should not be submitted as information, but a note should be made in the contact note about the discussion. For example, the source may tell a lurid tale of Tom White's activities with his lover which is circulating in the criminal world. The Handler may write an information submission to the effect that 'Tom White is having an affair with Jackie Black. This is annoying other gang members.' And in the contact note, the Handler may write: 'Source discussed in great detail the affair of Tom White. Handler's report material that has intelligence value but sometimes they have to listen to material that the source chooses to share, regardless of how uncomfortable it may be for the Handler.

Conclusion

The purpose of writing these groups of questions here is not to provide a comprehensive list of what we could ask a source. Each question raised above will lead to a further series of questions. If a Handler takes time to think about each question, they will come up with ten more, especially if they have sufficient knowledge of intelligence and covert operations. The key is for the Handler to develop their knowledge of the source's capabilities and task them for the benefit of the whole agency. The Handler knows they are there to provide a service to the entire agency at all levels and not just to satisfy the agenda of one unit. We lose the attitude that:

'I'm a drugs guy. I am not interested in any other sh*t.'[17]

Now that we know how to debrief a source and how to write it up, and all the things we should be asking, let us move on to discussing some of the other issues we are likely to encounter.

---

[17] Not my words!

8. Bringing It Together

I realized that my life was at risk; yet I knew that I could not permit an innocent man or woman to be targeted and murdered without trying everything in my power to stop it.

Fifty Dean Men Walking - Martin McGartland

Introduction

In this chapter, we will cover off on a final few points that will provide for a more robust way of managing human sources. We will look at some of the common issues that crop up and suggest solutions for them. The first of these is money.

Finance

There is a stereotypical view that cops are cheap! Like all stereotypes, there is an element of truth and when it comes to managing human sources, we can see a version of this play out regularly. In brief, law enforcement officers do not like to pay sources for providing information. There are several reasons for this, some of which have legitimacy, while others are entirely as a result of subjective values. First, many sources have extensive criminal backgrounds and make money from their criminal activities. Law enforcement officers do not like paying sources more money because the source is then profiting more, as a result of their criminality. This fails to take cognizance of the fact that if the source was not involved in criminality they would be of limited use, and the fact that they are being paid to betray the other criminals. Second, many officers have a sort of righteous indignation about paying anyone who would betray their friends or families. One can see the contradiction here, but that is the way our brain works. Third, senior managers, those responsible for allocating budgets, have no understanding of human source management and /or human motivation. Many would rather spend large sums of money on the surveillance of a target rather than pay a source who is already in a position to report much of the target's movements. They may resent paying a source a large sum of money, failing to take cognizance of how much money that source can save the agency. They want to have a source 'on the cheap' not realizing the potential risks this creates. Fourth, in a similar vein, they take no cognizance of the amount of effort a source may make to obtain information, nor the risks they take in doing so. Nothing shows a lack of knowledge of source management more than a failure to understand how to utilize money effectively in the management of human sources.

There are various ways that we can use money in the management of sources. First, we will consider issues around the salary for law enforcement officers. There needs to be 24/7 coverage for sources. A source may need to speak to a Handler at any time. A single Handler cannot be available 24/7. Therefore there has to be a central point where a source can make initial contact, where the call can be triaged. It is for the agency to decide how many Handlers/Controllers they will have on-call, at any one time. This will be based on the number of sources the agency has and the type of crime they are reporting upon. If there is a threat to a source, there must be a trained Handler/Controller who can evaluate and address that risk. It should be noted that Handlers or Controllers cannot speak to a source 'off duty' whether in person or on the phone. They should place themselves on duty, before speaking to a source. This prevents corruption where the Handler/Controller becomes overfamiliar with a source. It also means that the Handler is saying that they are fit to be on duty. For example, they cannot have consumed alcohol. Agencies also need to put in place a sufficient budget to allow for meetings outside of regular hours and at short notice. If sources can't be met safely, they should not be met. Sometimes this will require more than the deployment of two officers. These expenses will normally fall under central pay issues.

Second, is the equipment necessary to manage a source safely. This will include vehicles, computerized records, and other information technology, such as secure notebooks, recording devices, etc. Cellular phones are an ongoing expense. There needs to be a ready supply of 'burner' phones and numbers that are used exclusively for each source. Training relating to managing sources will also be included here. These expenses will fall under the annual budget for the agency for managing sources.

Third, are the expenses involved in managing the source. These will include ongoing expenses such as refreshments for the source, meals with the source, and hotel rooms for meetings. While most of these expenses are relatively small there has to be a budget to cover them. These expenses will be attributed to each source.

Fourth, are expenses incurred by the source in pursuit of their role as a source. This will include reimbursement of travel and phone bills. It may also include such aspects as paying for the rental or purchase of a car, being used by a source. Furthermore, in some cases, it may involve the purchase or rent of business premises to facilitate ongoing contact between the source and the targets. These expenses will be attributed to the individual source, that has incurred them.

Fifth, is ongoing financial assistance paid to the source. This will be decided by the Authorizing Officer, after consultation with the Controller and Handlers. It may take the form of a regular payment (a stipend[18]) allocated to the source every month or it may be paid on an occasional basis. The purpose of these payments is to compensate the source for the time that they have spent in gathering the information and for providing the agency with that information. Everyone expects to be paid fairly. Not paying a source is

_____

[18] A stipend is a fixed sum of money paid periodically for services rendered. This term avoids the use of the word 'salary' which conveys an employee/employer relationship.

counterproductive. Where a source is providing information over a prolonged period, a stipend is, in many cases, the most rational option. The Handlers know the amount of money available and can use it to motivate the source, making regular payments in line with productivity up to the identified limit. The bottom line is, we all need money to live, and if a source is getting it from their Handlers, they are more likely, to be more productive.

Sixth, is the paying of rewards for effort on the part of the source. Sometimes this can involve considerable sums of money. Rewards should be based on desired behavior and NOT on results. Where rewards are based on results what happens is that people take shortcuts to get results, and with sources, this will often involve unlawful activity. Ultimately, this can undermine a prosecution case. We want a source to give us good information and when they do, we should reward this. We should not say to the source if you give us X arrests you will get a reward. While the difference is subtle, it is critical. Payments by results are short-sighted and an outdated way of working. Handlers need to have an approximate idea of how much a source is likely to be rewarded. This is important to manage source expectations. Rewards should be realistic for the effort made and the risk that is undertaken. The goal of rewards is to motivate future similar behavior. Rewards should be decided by the Senior Responsible Officer in consultation with the Authorizing Officer.

All finance should be standardized throughout the agency. Sources in one region should be paid similar amounts to sources in other regions. Rewards should be consistent in size and should be paid promptly to the source, not months later. Rewards that are perceived by the source as unfair will motivate bad behavior and create unnecessary conflict for the Handlers. The poor manager will not see the problems this creates for the agency.

Paying sources is part of the 'cost of doing business.' Those involved need to realize this and adopt an objective view on it. Things that help in working out payments include considering: How many man-hours would it have taken police to find this out by traditional law enforcement methods? How much money was saved? Was there any alternative way that the information could have been obtained? The level that public confidence has been enhanced by the prevention of crime and or the recovery of contraband. And the golden guide: If you were the source how much would you think was a fair reward?

Providing gifts, etc.

There are many circumstances where it may not be suitable to pay money to a source. Alternatives include the provision of food vouchers, phone credit, or the payment of a bill. Also, it can be appropriate to provide gifts to a source to reward behavior. With all these options, similar records must be kept regarding the expenditure.

296

As an aside, the agency needs to have in place procedures that address the issue of the source providing Handlers with gifts. While the initial reaction may be that the Handlers must refuse any gift, this can be counterproductive. Where a source gives a gift to a Handler as a genuine gesture of goodwill refusing that gift is likely to be interpreted as offensive. Such procedures should facilitate the taking of a gift under given circumstances, while ensuring the Handler gains nothing personally.

Signing for money

Many agencies want sources to sign for any money they receive. The primary reasons for this are so that a) the Handler does not steal the money and b) the source does not allege they did not get the money. Working with cash always entails temptation. If the right structures for handling money are in place and officers are selected and trained properly for the role, then these steps are much more effective in controlling these risks. Most often making a source sign for money is at best a token gesture that masks other failings in processes.

Ethics

Ethics are the standards that an agency sets for the behavior of its officers. The agency head says 'This is how staff will behave. This type of behavior will not be tolerated.'

All those involved in managing sources should receive training in ethics and ethical decision making. This training should contain ethical theory and it should relate to specific source situations likely to be encountered. There are many situations where there are likely to be ethical dilemmas for the Source Management Team. Examples include, the use of a source to report on the activities of their spouse, the use of a source who has an extensive criminal history, and the use of a source who is under the age of eighteen.

Kidder (1995) provides a set of principles that can be used to resolve an ethical dilemma. Once learned they are easily used and very effective, in the source environment. He suggests that any ethical dilemma should be considered from three perspectives. The first approach suggests taking the *highest moral* perspective. This deontological position argues that one should always adopt the highest moral standpoint regardless of the consequences of adopting that position. This approach holds that some things are inherently wrong, regardless of the consequences that will occur. It does not matter how ethically good the consequences are, some choices are just wrong! While this position may be a very noble one, it arguably fails to recognize the real world, in which we live.

The second approach suggests taking a *care-based* perspective. This position takes the view that you should treat others as you would like to be treated. This approach is sometimes referred to as the 'golden rule' and has its basis in many religions. While this approach is very appealing, it fails to recognize that we can't be 'nice' all the time, to everyone, if we want to get a job done. The baker has to break eggs.

The third approach suggests taking an ***ends-based*** perspective. This position takes a utilitarian stance, arguing that the ends justify the means, and that one should do what is best for the greater number of people. Those that adopt such an approach are sometimes referred to as 'consequentialists'. They believe that choices are to be judged solely by the states of affairs they bring about. This approach is essentially a cost-benefit analysis which although attractive to many pragmatists, often fails to take cognizance of the views of others, especially those in the minority

By considering each of these perspectives and finding a balance in them, we are much more likely to make an ethically defendable position. Others may not agree with that decision, but we will be in a much better place to defend it.

Morals

While the term ***morals*** is often interpreted as meaning the same as ethics, drawing a distinction between the two aids understanding. Morals are personal values. '***I*** believe ***I*** should behave in this way. ***I*** think this is wrong.' There can sometimes be a conflict between the ethical standards of an agency and a person's morals. For example, an officer may believe they can have intimate relationships with anyone they choose, whereas this will undoubtedly conflict with the ethical standards of an agency when it comes to an intimate relationship between source and Handler. Conversely, the agency may wish the Handler to deceive the source in some way, for a legitimate purpose, while the Handler may feel that such a deception is morally wrong. Training around these types of issues is essential. It cannot be assumed that any officer understands ethics and morals unless, they have been properly trained in them.

Corruption

If you lie down with dogs, you will get up with fleas. While some sources are not involved in criminality, many are. When an agency asks Handlers to spend a considerable amount of time with sources, those Handlers are regularly exposed to circumstances where corruption can easily occur. The risk of corruption occurring with sources is high and one of the main reasons for having dedicated Handlers manage sources, is to mitigate that risk. The more officers that are exposed to the risk of corruption, the greater the chances of it occurring are, and the more serious the corruption is likely to be.

When we train Handlers properly, they are much more likely to identify behavior that could lead to corruption occurring. In addition, some officers are more easily manipulated than others. We want to identify officers who are more vulnerable during the training process. Eliminating those unsuitable for source management is another critical element to mitigate the risk. Controllers also play a vital part by intrusive supervision. If a Handler knows that corrupt behave is more likely to be detected, they are less likely to engage in it.

Another important element that the right training provides for Handlers is self-awareness. If we are aware of our vulnerabilities, we can take steps to guard against them being exploited. If we think for example, that no one is smarter than us, then when we meet the criminal that is, they will manipulate us and we will never see it coming.

Corruption will come in many different forms and these need to be clearly identified in the risk assessment process and managed accordingly. Corruption will take hold easily in bad systems and thrive there. Blaming corruption on 'one bad apple' only masks the underlying causes and rarely addresses the problem.

Buy-bust operations and controlled purchases

'Buy-bust' is a technique that is often used by those involved in narcotics operations. At its worst, it involves sending a source to 'buy' drugs to verify that there are drugs at a particular location. As soon as the drugs have been purchased the Investigators 'bust' the dealer. Short of putting a large neon sign on the source's head that reads 'informant', it is hard to think of a more obvious way to identify someone who is assisting law enforcement.

While the example given may illustrate the crudest use of the technique, this exploitation of human sources unnecessarily places the source's life in danger and adds little to combat the greater drug threat. Sending the source in to make a controlled purchase is often done as a means of verifying that there are drugs in the premises, thus satisfying the need for corroboration of intelligence to gain a search warrant. It is in many ways lazy policing and it continues unabated because officers do not know how to use sources more productively and/ or how to use intelligence to satisfy a judge and obtain a warrant. The problem is compounded by the fact that prosecutors don't understand the risks involved. All they want to do is make a case that stands up in court.

Also, often there is little additional information extracted from the source. 'Make these buys for me then you are good to go.' The Investigator moves from bust to bust with no long-term strategy. Little if any attempt is made to use the source to gain a more comprehensive intelligence picture, one where long-term operations can be carried out to combat the supply routes and major dealers. Adding to this problem is the fact that because no time is invested in building a relationship with the source, the knowledge that the source has in their head is never extracted and submitted for intelligence purposes.

Controlled operations are fraught with danger to the source, the officers involved, and to the agency and are generally of little benefit to an overall counter-drugs strategy. They are for the most part just a numbers game sadly sometimes played with a callous disregard for the life of another human being. Too often officers are injured or killed carrying out such operations because of the gung-ho approach that is adopted.

'Stop Snitching'

Many communities are openly hostile to members of the community assisting law enforcement. Most law enforcement agencies will have to deal with this issue to a greater or lesser extent. While some of the causes of this problem may vary from place to place many overarching elements are similar. To gain an understanding of the issues we will consider one concerted campaign to reduce citizens passing information to the police. This particular campaign is present across the USA, but because of the prevalence of American culture, some of the terminology from it has spread to other English-speaking nations. It is referred to as 'Stop Snitchin' with 'snitchin' being an abbreviation of the word snitching and that being a derogatory term for informing. It is often accompanied by a picture of a rat and with phrases such as 'Snitches get stitches.'

The campaign has its origins in Baltimore. It has caused significant harm to the ability of law enforcement to collect evidence and intelligence from citizens, particularly from minority or 'hard to reach' communities. Without delving too much into the history of the campaign, it can be said to be motivated by several factors including the mistrust of the police and the perceived racism of the police. It is fed by a misguided 'code of honor' that one should not betray one's one community regardless of the cost to that community.

The perception of the police being against, or at war with, a particular community plays a part. This perception is often promoted by the criminals living within that community. The failure of police to protect those who do provide information adds to the problem. This is especially damaging where sources are seen as being disposable and it is combined with a lack of adequate witness protection type schemes to protect sources whose identity has been exposed.

The problem is exacerbated by a sense of injustice that minor offenders are being 'snitched on' and prosecuted while the 'king-pins' do the snitching and are allowed to walk free by the police. Undoubtedly this happens because performance is based on criteria such as the number of persons charged, as opposed to who was charged and what damage that did to the criminality.

While this is far from a comprehensive list of reasons why the campaign has been successful, there is a lot that law enforcement can do to overcome it, as it can do with any 'hard to reach community':

Effective community policing is a good start. The agency needs to get good officers on the ground, into the communities and let those officers build trust. Psychology says: 'if we trust someone, we are more likely to give them information.' Far too often community policing has been allowed to become a dumping ground for those officers who don't want to work or are unsuitable for any type of work. Community officers are the agency's public face and what they say and do impacts on how the community reacts. Furthermore, care must be taken not to allow some over-zealous detective to undermine the investment these officers have made.

Law enforcement needs to put in place structures to protect those who provide information. Far too often a person gives information and within days their identity becomes known and their role as a 'confidential informant' is widely reported throughout their community. This begs the question, where is the confidentiality? Why would anyone in their right mind give information?

Police commanders should publicize the necessity for the community to assist law enforcement including highlighting the parasitic nature of crime gangs and emphasizing the close working relationships that law enforcement has with community and faith leaders in that community. Again, this assumes that the legwork has been done and such relationships are in place. In addition, hopefully, law enforcement is not perceived as being racist or prejudiced against one community or one group.

No law enforcement officer should be allowed to use the terms 'snitch' or 'rat' or any such derogatory term. All this does is add credibility to the campaign. The use of such language by journalists, lawyers, or whoever should be challenged by law enforcement, just as they would challenge the use of any other inappropriate language. Citizens should be continually praised for having the courage to come forward and provide information that helps their community.

Where an incident of a particular nature has aroused community outrage then law enforcement must grab the opportunity to gather information about the incident and to build relationships that increase the likelihood of obtaining information in the future. While some may critique this from an ethical standpoint, the reality is that law enforcement must take every opportunity that arises to build bridges with these types of community. It is better that some good should come out of a tragedy than nothing at all.

Human sources come in many different guises. Some of the best sources are community leaders, who work with law enforcement, in a covert way for the betterment of their community and to protect their community from crime.

Participation in crime

Some sources are going to commit crime while registered as sources. No matter how many times they are told, no matter how many terms and conditions they sign, they will keep on doing what they have done all their lives. That is the reality. The nature of the crimes the Handler believes the source will continue to be involved in needs to be written in the risk documents. It is then for the Authorizing Officer to decide if the benefits of managing this source outweigh the risks. It must be seen that the law enforcement agency is not condoning criminality nor is turning a blind eye to it. If the source is caught doing something criminal, then that must be dealt with in the normal way. Burying heads in the sand or claiming some sort of corporate ignorance of the situation is unacceptable.

If a source is going to take part in crime, at the behest of an agency, that activity and any associated activity such as surveillance must be approved by the Senior Responsible Officer. The source's role must be clearly documented, as should how their participation in the crime will further the investigation. Before approving such activity, the Senior Responsible Officer should convene a Strategic Advisory Group meeting to discuss the benefits and risks involved in the investigation and the source's involvement in it. This is to ensure that if one part of the plan fails the necessary safeguards are in place and the source is not left exposed. These meetings must be attended by the Controller and a Handler, as they are best placed to articulate the capabilities of the source.

Using interpreters

Language difficulties can arise with some sources. Where there is insufficient knowledge of a common shared language in which to communicate, it may be necessary to use an interpreter to facilitate the interaction. Assuming that the interpreter is fluent in the language and if they properly trained and briefed, upon their role, the use of an interpreter will cause minimal disruption. Everyone involved just needs to be that bit more patient. Things will go slower. Where the interpreter is from a similar background, they may well have a greater knowledge of the culture to which the source is referring to, than the Handler. This can add value. However, care must be taken if the interpreter and source are from small communities. They may come into contact with each other outside of the role, or there may be close connections back in the country of origin. Good interpreters can also interpret, not only the literal meaning of a statement, but also the intent and emotion contained in the words used.

The establishment of rapport and the use of some other techniques are made difficult when working through an interpreter. Also, the ability of the Handler to interpret the truthfulness of the source through the analysis of word usage, and the nuances of their speech, becomes limited. However, the Handler should continue to monitor the body language of the source as clues will remain here. It should also be born in mind that the interpreter will have their biases that can influence how the dialogue is interpreted and this can impact the relationship.

Recording of meetings when using an interpreter takes on an added level of importance for two reasons. First, it provides a resource for the interpreter to go over later in case they have missed something. Things often get lost in translation. The interpreter can listen to the recording and correct any errors they may have made. Second, if there is any doubt as to the competence or the integrity of the interpreter, alternative translation can be obtained. This is a safety mechanism that should be employed when using a new interpreter for the first meetings.

Proactive recruitment

Proactive recruitment of human sources is a method used to recruit more sources and specifically high-value human sources. In essence, it is as the name says. It is about going out and asking people to become sources as opposed to waiting for someone to volunteer. The traditional paradigm has been that a criminal will want to 'work of a charge' or 'pay off a debt' or 'wants vengeance against some other criminal.' This then motivates them to talk to law enforcement for a limited duration.

The proactive paradigm changes this. The Handlers take responsibility for identifying potential sources and then making an approach on the person to ask them to become a source. When this is done properly, it is a highly effective way of recruiting more sources and managing them more effectively.

It relies on two key elements. First, the Handler has to be able to identify who is likely to respond to an approach and what that person's motives would be to speak with law enforcement. This requires a sufficiently high level of knowledge of the psychology involved. Analysts can be used to build a comprehensive picture of a person's lifestyle. This will help in identifying potential motives. The second thing is that the Handler has to have the interpersonal skills to rapidly build a relationship in a fluid situation. Upskilling officers to this level, takes time. Despite the benefits of it, few agencies are aware of the relevant theories and fewer have the knowledge to deliver the training needed to the required standard. This is especially true when it comes to recruiting high-value targets.

Having said that, agencies can be much more proactive in recruiting sources. Unplanned opportunities arise to speak to potential sources. Things that are likely to get results include Handlers engaging more regularly with anyone that could provide the information that is needed. For example, a Handler may observe a well-known criminal in a police station having been arrested for impaired driving: 'Hey, I am Mia. I am a detective here. I thought I would pop in and see how things were going.' The officer then engages in social chat only, creating a none threatening ambiance. This is the start of contact with the potential source. The more times the officer tries this, the greater their skills will become, provided they have the aptitude.

Similarly, using uniform officers to identify people within the community who have assisted police in the past can also bring results. Often the uniform officer commences a relationship of sorts but does not know how to maximize its potential. Here the Handler can step in and bring their skill set into play for the benefit of the entire agency, while at the same time affording greater protection to the person who is being helpful.

The more knowledge Handlers have of the techniques involved in proactive recruitment the more opportunities are created. The capacity of the agency grows exponentially and criminal organizations that were once perceived as being invincible become a lot more vulnerable.

Psychology

This book has mentioned a limited amount about psychology. However, understanding the psychology involved in a source relationship is critical if that relationship is to be productive and have duration. Understanding how people think and why they do things is critical at all ranks of the agency involved in source management. In source management, we are continually trying to predict human behavior. This is difficult to do at the best of times. Without sufficient knowledge of psychology, it is all but impossible.

Day zero

If we are building a new source management system, it is good to have a Day Zero. This is the day from which all sources will be managed under the new system. On Day Zero, no source is being managed outside of a Dedicated Source Unit and the status of all existing sources has been reviewed. Those that are deemed suitable to be retained are reregistered and authorized and those that do not reach the grade are deregistered and no longer met. All the previous records are retained for an identified period. Having a Day Zero provides reassurance to all involved especially the Chief, that there is nothing that they are unaware of that is going to come out of the woodwork at a later date and bite them. Furthermore, if there has been a problem identified steps can be taken to reduce the potential impact of that problem.

Managing knowledge

The only reason that this book has come about is because officers have shared their knowledge of things that have worked for them and mistakes that have been made by them. When we learn things, we need to have a way of capturing them and sharing them with fellow professionals. There is no need for them to learn it for themselves nor is there a need for them to repeat the mistakes we have made. Controllers should take it upon themselves to share such knowledge with others in the agency either through discussion or training. If the agency has permanent training staff keeping them up to speed with good practice is important. Equally, sharing with other agencies will help them.

Conclusion

The effective use of human sources, as outlined in this book, represents value for money. More often than not the problem in realizing this value for money is not with the using sources as a concept. It is the fact that agencies do not invest in building the structures needed, for the long-term effective management of sources.

Often, agencies have hundreds of registered sources on their books, many of whom have provided information on a one-off basis and then have been left on the records without ever being used again. Officers talk about having many sources but never meet with them. We create an illusion of being busy. We create the myth that we are involved in intelligence-led policing.

There is a process of natural attrition with human sources. They move away to different towns. They lose their access, or they cease their involvement in criminality. Sources are managed to satisfy short-term goals and then abandoned. Handlers switch roles and the source is of no use to them in their current role. If the agency has effective source structures, sources stay more productive for longer periods and the agency gets more information. Handlers become more professional and they recruit more and better sources. More crimes are prevented, and offenders are brought to justice.

It the agency is facing a terrorism problem and they are not proactively recruiting and managing sources against this threat, then there is little chance of curtailing the terrorist's activities. There is little any terrorist organization can do to combat the activities of properly managed sources. When sources are proactively recruited, the terrorist organization has nowhere to start in looking for the source.

There are some senior figures in law enforcement that have misguided and ill-informed views on managing sources. Some do not like using sources at all. They have an obsessive-like aversion to them. 'I won't sully my hands with the beastly creatures.' This is often driven by risk aversion or adopting a highly subjective moral stance. Others are cavalier in their approach to managing them. Their idea of motivation is 'Get them by the balls and keep squeezing.' This approach lacks ethics and effectiveness, and some would say any humanity. And finally, there are others who despite all the evidence to the contrary, all the corruption and the lost lives, still think that anyone can manage sources. They think that because they did it once upon a time, that 'any idiot can do it' without actually thinking through the ramifications of what they have just admitted. Unfortunately, these officers, because of their position of power, undermine all the good that has been done by more junior officers or their predecessors. Their attitude to source management is just a symptom of their attitude in general. These are people that keep policing in the past.

Fortunately, there are also many more good senior officers who genuinely want to improve how their agency manages human sources, to raise levels of professionalism and work in more ethical ways.

This book is about professionalizing the way that human sources are managed. While most law

314

enforcement agencies manage sources, many lag behind in having proper systems to get the most out of them. What has been presented here, are tried and tested methods to protect the agency, the public, the officers involved, and the source. There is no downside save for a bit of work in setting the structures up and a few bruised egos. The tools you need to get started are here. What you do with them is up to you.

But let us not forget, these are the basics. Adherence to what is suggested creates competence. There is a whole lot more to learn on our journey to excellence. Take this knowledge that others have worked hard for. Use it to do what you took an oath to do. Serve and protect all without fear or favor.

And the next time you hear someone talk about 'rats' or 'snitches', just remember there are a lot of people safer in their bed tonight because some rat or snitch risked their life to provide the information that keeps them safe.

Author's Endnote

I realize that for some readers there may be frustration that I have not explored issues around 'Fieldcraft' in greater detail. First, if the reader is searching for more details on the psychology involved, and they are a member of a law enforcement agency then contact us about our publication The Human Source Management System - The use of psychology in the management of human sources. You will find a lot of what you want there.

When it comes to talking about Fieldcraft in terms of keeping all involved safe, this is a topic that needs to be kept within the law enforcement and intelligence communities. Why tell the bad guys how we do our business? These things are best left for the classroom where the training can be adapted to the operational environment and the risks that exist. However, if you want to get in contact to discuss any point, please do not hesitate to do so.

My job is done here. I have given you the knowledge that was shared with me. Now that you know what you should be doing, it is down to you to lead the change.

About the Author

Paperwork is not his strong point. It took ten years and a global pandemic to write this book. And while there are probably lots of excuses for it taking so long, undoubtedly the lack of anyone standing over him with a big stick in one hand and a beer in the other, meant that there was limited motivation to complete it.

So now instead of him whining that no one listens to what he says, he can now add, that no one has bothered their ass to even read it either.

And in the interests of full disclosure, there may be a few things in here that he says you should do, but where he did the opposite. He never said he was perfect, but he has tried to learn from his (many) mistakes.

References

Billingsley, R. (2009) Risk Management. In Billingsley, R. (Ed.) Covert Human Intelligence Sources. The unlovely face of police work. England. Waterside Press.

Buckley J. F (2015) Managing Intelligence Buckley, J. (2013) Managing Intelligence: A Guide for Law Enforcement Professionals. Boca Raton CRC Press

Buckley, J.F. (2009) Managing Information from the Public. In: Billingsley, R. (Ed.) Covert Human Intelligence Sources. The unlovely face of police work. England: Waterside Press.

Buckley, J.F (2008) Invest Now or Pay Later – The management of risk in covert law enforcement. London: HSM Publishing

Buckley, J.F.(2006) The Human Source Management System The use of psychology in the Management of Human Intelligence Sources HSM Publishing London

Connolly, D.A. and Price, H.L. (2006) Children's suggestibility for an instance of a repeated event versus a unique event: The degree of association between variable options. Journal of Experimental Child Psychology 93. 207-203.

Festinger, L. (1957) A theory of cognitive dissonance. Stanford, CA: Stanford University Press.

318

Fisher, R.D., Geiselman, R.E. and Raymond, D.S. (1987) Critical Analysis of Police Interview Techniques. Journal of Police Science and Administration 15 177-185.

Geiselman, R. E., Fisher, R. P., Firstenberg, I. Hutton, L. A., Sullivan, S. J., Avetissain, I. V., Prosk, A. L. (1984). Enhancement of eyewitness memory: An empirical evaluation of the cognitive interview. Journal of Police Science and Administration, 12[1], 74-80.

Henry, P., Rajakaruna, N., Crous, C., Buckley, J., (2019), Key attributes of an effective human source Handler: Implications for Handler selection and training. The Police Journal: Theory, Practice and Principles,

Kebell, M., Milne, R Wagstaff, G. (1997): The Cognitive Interview: A survey of its forensic effectiveness. Psychology, Crime and Law 5. pp101-116.

Kidder, R. M. (1995). How good people make tough choices. New York: Simon & Schuster.

Lamb, M.E., Orbach, Y., Sternberg, K.J., Hershkowitz, I. and Horoitz, D. (2000) Accuracy of Investigators' Verbatim notes of their Forensic Interviews with Alleged Child Abuse Victims. Law and Human Behaviour 24. 699-708.

Melton, A. (1963) Implications of Short-Term Memory for a General Theory of Memory Journal of Verbal learning and Verbal Behaviour 2 1-21

Milne, R. and Bull, R. (2003) Interviewing by the Police. In Carson D. and Bull R. (Eds.) Handbook of Psychology in Legal Contexts. Wiley. England.

Natapoff, A. (2009) Snitching - Criminal Informants and the Erosion of American Justice. New York: New York University Press.

Rogers, E., (2003) Diffusion of Innovations, 5th Edition. Simon and Schuster. UK

Reid, C. and Buckley, J. (2005) Human Source Management – A better approach to managing human intelligence sources. Home Office Police Research Awards. UK: Crown Copyright.

Tulving, E., and Thomson, D.M. (1973) Encoding Specifity and Retrieval Processes in Episodic Memory. Psychological review 80. pp 352-373.

Tulving, E. (1991) Concepts of Human Memory. In Suire, L.R., Weinberger, N.M., Lynch, G., and McGaugh, J.L. (Eds.) Memory: Organisation and Locus of Change. New York. Oxford University Press.

BY THE SAME AUTHOR

The Human Source Management System – The use of psychology in the management of human intelligence sources. (2006)

[Available only to law enforcement through website]

Invest Now or Pay Later – The management of risk in covert law enforcement. (2008)

Managing Intelligence – A guide for law enforcement professionals. (2015)

Understanding Ego Defense Mechanisms: A guide for educators. (2019)

Why: Understanding Motive and Motivation (2020)

For more information on these books, or about training, visit our website:
www.hsmtraining.com